KIDS WITH ZIP

JOANNE LANDY AND KEITH BURRIDGE

KIDS
with ZIP

A practical resource for educators and parents
to develop active children ages 3-12

Prentice
Hall

Copyright © 2002 Pearson Education Australia Pty Limited

Pearson Education Australia
Unit 4, Level 2
14 Aquatic Drive
Frenchs Forest NSW 2086

Acquisitions Editor: Diane Gee-Clough
Project Editor: Jane Roy
Copy Editor: Janice Keynton
Cover and internal design: R.T.J. Klinkhamer
Typeset by Midland Typesetters, Maryborough VIC

Printed in Malaysia, CLP

4 5 06 05

ISBN 1 74009 739 4

National Library of Australia
Cataloguing-in-Publication data

Landy, Joanne.
  Kids With Zip: a practical resource for promoting active
  children ages 3–12.

  ISBN 1 74009 739 4

  1. Physical fitness for children. 2. Children – Health and
  hygiene. 3. Children – Nutrition. I. Burridge, Keith.
  II. Title.

  613.7042

An imprint of Pearson Education

Contents

PART 2 50 KIDS WITH ZIP SESSIONS

About the authors

Joanne M. Landy earned a B.Ed. degree, graduating with Great Distinction from the University of Regina, Saskatchewan, Canada in 1974. She also completed a postgraduate international Physical Education (P.E.) study course through Concordia University in Montreal, Quebec, and in 1999 a Personal Trainer course through Renouf Fitness Academy in Perth, Western Australia.

Joanne's professional background includes 10 years of secondary teaching in Physical Education/Health and Mathematics; 10 years of specialist teaching in primary Physical Education and Health, as well as several years of University demonstration teaching in P.E. methodology and pedagogy programs in the Canadian school system. In 1988 Joanne was also part of the leadership team for the National Youth Foundation Fitness Camp in Los Angeles, California.

Joanne has presented at major conferences in the U.S.A., Australia and New Zealand. She also has facilitated many P.E. workshops for primary/secondary teachers in the field and for teacher-training programs. For the past three years Joanne has been lecturing at Murdoch University, Faculty of Education, in the primary Physical Education teacher-training program in Perth.

She has co-authored several elementary and lower secondary P.E. resources in the areas of movement, dance, fitness, gross and fine motor skills development, teaching strategies and methods, including the 'Ready-To-Use PE Activities Series (K–9)' (co-authored with her late husband Max Landy, 1994) and 'The New Motor Skills Series' (co-authored with Keith Burridge, May 2000), a teaching, assessing and remediation program.

Joanne now resides with her children Max Jr and Nikki in Perth and operates a Lifestyle Education consulting business which provides in-depth workshops and inservicing in Physical Education at all levels, including University P.E. teacher-training programs. Joanne has been instrumental in developing and coordinating youth activity-based programs including a 'Tune Up Kids' program for young children ages 5–12 years, focusing on the development of fundamental movement skills and fitness; a Basketball Development Program for 6–12-year-olds; and a program of motivation and self-esteem for teenage girls (13–18 years called 'On The Move'. She also has initiated several 'Tune Up' programs for adults and provided team-building and motivational sessions for school staffs, corporate business groups and other community interest groups.

She maintains an active lifestyle in Perth centring on her own personal fitness, tennis, golfing, dancing, jogging, wave skiing, gardening, playing guitar and writing.

Keith R. Burridge earned a Dip. Ed from Nedlands Secondary Teachers College, followed by a B.P.E. degree (1978) and M.Ed. from the University of Western Australia, Perth. Keith's professional background includes 15 years as a secondary Physical Education and Science teacher, 5 years as a primary physical education specialist and 4 years of special education working with children with movement difficulties. From 1995–97 he was employed by the Department of Education of Western Australia (Perth) as a school Development Officer in Physical Education and was responsible for the professional development of P.E. in over 80 schools. He has represented Australia at the elite level in canoeing.

Keith was one of the key writers for the Western Australian Department of Education's 1998 Fundamental Movement Skills Package. He has lectured at Notre Dame College of Education in Fremantle, W.A., and Murdoch University in Perth, W.A., and facilitated programs for early childhood education. Keith has presented F.M.S. and best practices in teaching workshops throughout Western Australia. He is the co-author with Joanne Landy of the 3 book Motor Skills series. As an F.M.S. specialist, Keith has contributed to the writing of a book called *Why Bright Children Fail* (Hammond, 1996). He is also the designer for a K–3 computer assessment package for identifying children at an early age who have coordination problems. This program is in operation in over 400 schools in Western Australia.

Presently, Keith is teaching at Willeton Senior High School in Perth and piloting a special program to work with children at educational risk.

PART ONE:

WHAT YOU NEED TO KNOW

About this book

The purpose of this book is manyfold: to provide quality movement experiences for young children (from ages 3–12) that enhance listening skills, reaction and alertness; to develop spatial and body awareness, motor memory, and overall body management and coordination; to develop fitness, both health- and skill-related; to foster cooperation, fair play and social interaction at the developmentally appropriate age level; and to foster a healthy happy 'habit' and 'attitude' in young children which will carry over into active teenagers and active adults. The idea is to literally 'hook' young children into wanting to be active at as early an age as possible! Early intervention is the key to prevention in a 'child-centred' approach to health and fitness.

Kids with Zip aims to reach anyone and everyone who is involved with young children: early childhood educators teaching young children in pre-primary school programs; parents who are keen to develop well-rounded, fit children; recreational instructors and sports club coaches training young children; day-care educational carers looking after children in out-of-school care programs; primary generalist teachers and physical education specialists in lower and middle primary schools.

How to use this book

Kids with Zip is divided into two parts. The first part provides the user with pertinent information, concisely presented, about the characteristics of young children between the ages of 3–12 essential understandings and principles of sound quality fitness, good nutrition and motor coordination; and how to use this knowledge to provide effective practical ideas for reaching young children and instilling a wish to be active. The authors have also included a section on addressing children with special needs, such as asthma, sensory impairment and physical or intellectual disabilities.

Part 2 is written for the purpose of providing a plethora of 'hands-on' ideas for developing and fostering physically active children. The 50 Kids with Zip Sessions contain over 600 practical and valuable child-centred ideas that can be implemented immediately into any existing program. Children will be more likely to develop positive fitness *attitudes* and *habits* if they are involved in enjoyable, developmentally appropriate movement experiences; the overriding factor being that the child's experience be an enjoyable one, with praise and encouragement providing the essential feedback.

The 50 Kids with Zip Sessions provide fitness ideas for indoor and outdoor play, confined space play, seasonal activities and special events, such as birthday parties, sports club get-togethers and playgroup functions. 'Active' ideas are provided for the individual child, partner play, small group and large group play where appropriate, and are progressively presented to accommodate a range of 3–12 years.

Throughout the book relevant 'Fit Tips' occur which can be used as discussion points at the developmentally appropriate age level. Also, several suggestions for innovative and manipulative equipment are presented, including ideas for making some of this equipment. *Kids with Zip* is fully illustrated using simple 'action figures' which show the desirable movement and assist in the explanation of the activity or game.

Safety pointers are included as needed with each of the activities.

Overview of Kids with Zip Sessions

• **Sessions 1–6** provide many activities for developing the basic skills needed for spatial and body awareness, enhancing and improving motor memory, balance and coordination; signals for developing and enhancing listening skills, alertness and reaction responses; and body management exercises that develop stopping and starting responses, falling and recovery, and postural activities.

• **Sessions 7–31** provide 25 Fit Session ideas that develop and foster the health- and skill-related components of fitness, with particular emphasis on aerobic ability, strength through weight-bearing activities and flexibility.

• **Sessions 32–34** provide activities for outdoor play and seasonal conditions, such as winter activities of ice-skating and tobogganing, and water activities.

• **Sessions 35–36** focus on activities that can be done on rainy days or in limited space and provide ideas for integration of other concepts, such as maths and reading.

• **Active Session 37** includes ideas and activities that build on colour/number recognition and association, maths concepts, road safety and Australian geography.

• **Sessions 38–41** include many tag-type and low-organised games that can be played with partners and small or large groups of children.

• From this follow **Sessions 42–43** providing more ideas for functions, such as birthday parties.

• **Session 44** provides combative play activities that further build on the skill-related fitness components of agility, strength, balance, coordination, speed, reaction time and, to a certain extent, power.

• **Sessions 45–47** provide many ideas for getting children to move to music, including using musical instruments which can be commercially purchased or home-made.

• **Session 48** provides indoor and outdoor fitness circuit ideas in which the children rotate through a series of activities that focus

on aerobic activity by using a variety of locomotion movements, overall body strength, balance and coordination, and agility—all in an enjoyable and cooperative effort.
* Finally, **Sessions 49–50** provide quiet-time activities fostering concentration ability, cooperation, body management, body awareness and more flexibility.

To the parents

The content of this book will provide you, as parents, with a variety of quality movement experiences that you and your child(ren) can do together. Acquiring competence and confidence in movement will enhance children's overall coordination and nurture their self-esteem. Equally as important, children will build up their fitness to develop good aerobic capacity, strength, flexibility, speed, agility, alertness and reaction.

From an early age children need to acquire good spatial awareness, both in personal and general space, body awareness (body image), and to learn to move with effort and in relationship with others. *Children need to learn to move but, at the same time, they need to move to learn.* Fundamental movement skills are the building blocks of all movement. They are the foundation for skills that your child will use later in life to pursue recreational or competitive sporting activities. They include the locomotion movements of walking, running, dodging, jumping and landing, leaping, hopping, skipping, sliding, balancing, starting and stopping, and the non-locomotion movements of climbing, hanging, swinging, pushing, pulling and rotating. Fundamental motor skills (object control skills) of rolling, throwing and catching, kicking and striking can then be developed.

The established fact is that children, who are physically active from an early age and receive positive, enjoyable and successful movement experiences in this early stage of their life, will continue to engage in and pursue physical activity on a regular basis as adults throughout their lifetime. The benefits in terms of wellbeing are physiological, psychological (emotional stability), social, vocational and academic.

This book targets the 3–12-year-old child and focuses on the best movement experiences that you can have with children. You will enjoy being actively involved too and can benefit from quality time well-invested in the children's welfare. These activities have been progressively organised with indoor and outdoor suggestions, including limited space or rainy day activities, seasonal activities, tagging-type activities, large group and party group activities, integrated activities, concentration and combative-type activities, rhythm and dance activities, balancing and body management, motor memory activities, and spatial and body awareness activities, plus 25 different Fit Sessions. Enjoy!

What teachers/parents need to know

10 essential understandings

1. Make fitness fun!

How you as an adult look at fitness is different from how children perceive fitness. Children are not mini-adults. Children simply obtain their fitness by doing activities that they enjoy. As soon as we as parents impose 'training' on them, we create a battle of resistance. Young children's interests can be short term and quick changing. They have an inconsistent attention span. They tire easily, but recover quickly. Therefore, be reasonable in the degree of physical exertion demanded.

2. Everyone plays!

Play is fundamental to life and contributes to the overall development of children. Play is a significant means for children to explore, express and discover many aspects of life; to learn and to find real value and meaning in the experience; to develop fitness and skills; and to learn 'social graces'.

3. Understand the 'want–fear' premise

We as adults may work on our fitness out of 'fear' of a heart attack, of gaining weight and acquiring hypokinetic diseases of a modern civilisation. Some of us engage in fitness workouts because we do indeed enjoy activity as a lifestyle pursuit; others become addicted, even obsessive. But children are too detached from the 'fear' factor; therefore, we as teachers/parents need to develop the 'want to' attitude at an early age. This is best achieved by making activity always enjoyable for them.

4. Know the importance of body management

From an early age children need to develop an appreciation and awareness of their bodies and what they can do in a childlike way. Children who are poorly coordinated or lack general overall coordination do not have appropriate movement skills and will not develop good fitness. For example, children who can't run or who do not run properly, who keep falling over or running into things and getting hurt, are hindered significantly in their aerobic development.

Children need to be able to manage their bodies. A prerequisite to any fitness or activity program is that children feel comfortable with moving. Children who do not like to be active because movement becomes difficult for them, will have a tendency to become overweight, lethargic, have poor aerobic endurance and coordination problems. Overweight children, children who lack coordination, children who lack flexibility will look for excuses to be inactive, and this will have significant implications for their growth and development, general fitness and social development. Therefore, we must impact early—with fun enjoyable coordination activities.

5. Be aware of kids' growth and development

Children's bones have not developed to maturity. Movement is needed for development of strong bones and muscles; therefore, it is important that children experience developmentally appropriate activities for their age group.

6. Be a positive role model

Children learn by example. Children learn by watching you. They will mimic your actions, whether you are a cycling enthusiast or a 'couch potato'. Be a positive role model by being enthusiastic and joining in when and where possible. Children need your approval. Encourage, praise and provide constructive feedback; but don't push or become overbearing.

7. See fitness as the big picture

Fitness needs to be viewed as a holistic experience. The important point to emphasise is that physical fitness is only one part of health and wellbeing, which also includes nutrition, play, mental health, quality sleep, relaxation and emotional health.

For children to be functioning at their best, there must be a balance of all these components. They are all 'life keys' in the big picture. Physical fitness is developed from exercise and activity; but physical fitness needs to be partnered with good nutrition. Both exercise and good nutrition contribute to overall health—one without the other creates an imbalance:

GENERAL PHYSICAL HEALTH = REGULAR EXERCISE + GOOD NUTRITION!

Physical fitness has two components:

Health-related	Skill-related
Cardiovascular	Speed
Muscle strength	Power
Muscle endurance	Agility
Flexibility	Balance
Body composition	Coordination
	Reaction time

· Health-related components focus on developing good health and preventing diseases and other problems resulting from inactivity ('hypokinetic diseases').

Skill-related components focus on skills and developing ability to perform well in overall movement, sports, dance and gymnastics. But *coordination* is often the key that unlocks the door to activity and fitness. Thus the importance of incorporating health-related components with skill-related components cannot be understated.

This book provides 25 Fit Sessions that have been divided into 3 areas: aerobic, strength and flexibility. Within each of these sessions is a deliberate attempt to mix health-related components with skill-related components.

8. Be aware of exercise do's and don'ts

Always 'warm up' children first with low–moderate activity. Movements should be gentle and rhythmical, then gradually increased in intensity. Try to use all the major muscle groups in the warm-up activity.

Never stretch cold muscles. Avoid ballistic movements when stretching. Avoid exercises that hyper-extend any joint areas. No massive weight-bearing exercises should be used. Children can use their own body weight to develop strength.

9. Provide a variety of activities

Make activity the 'name of the game', but vary the intensity. Make the activity fun, interesting, stimulating and motivating! You could even provide an incentive such as going to the water slides, to the movies or on a downhill ski trip.

10. Need to develop a 'knowing' attitude and an exercise habit

Need to develop a 'knowing' attitude, not necessarily a 'fitness' attitude. Get children used to being active, used to doing exercise, and 'in the know' of *why* exercise is so good for them! Consistency becomes a habit. There is a need to establish an 'activity routine schedule' with children. But don't mistake consistency with regularity. You may not always have the time or the opportunity to do an activity session with children at the same time each day, so be realistic about the time constraints and be flexible within consistency.

Characteristics of being 3

Three-year-olds are in a world of awakening—full of curiosity and wonder, busily exploring their world, watching, observing and imitating. At this developmental stage they are interested in perfecting motor skills and will often spend lengthy periods of time riding their favourite tricycle or going up and down the slide at the park. They will often repeat activities or may do and undo activities such as putting a puzzle together. They do not understand 'yesterday' and 'tomorrow' like adults do, and have little memory for past events.

Physical development
- Can brush teeth, wash and dry hands, and hold a glass in one hand
- Sleeps 10–12 hours through most nights, without bed-wetting—but the occasional accident still occurs
- Girls are almost toilet trained; boys still in toilet learning stage; but both can use toilet with some help

- Can feed self with spoon and small fork, often butter bread with knife, but still with some spilling
- Interested in handling food and cooking procedures
- Can put on shoes, but not tie shoelaces
- Can dress self with some help (zippers, buttons or snaps)
- Can stand, balance and hop on one foot
- Can walk a short distance on tiptoes and walk on a line
- Can jump over a low hurdle and jump with both feet
- Can climb up steps, alternating feet, and slide down by self
- Can pedal a tricycle
- Can stack 5–7 blocks
- Tries to catch a large ball
- Can throw a ball overhead
- Can kick a ball forwards

Intellectual development
- Can talk in 3–5 word sentences and so that 75–80% of their speech can be understood
- Will sometimes stumble over words, but usually not a sign of stuttering
- Enjoys repeating words and sounds
- Listens attentively to short stories and reading from a book
- Is able to tell simple stories from pictures or books
- Enjoys repeating simple rhymes
- Enjoys singing and can carry a simple tune
- Recognises common everyday sounds
- Understands 'now, soon and later' and remembers what happened yesterday
- Asks who, what, where and why questions
- Can put together a 6-piece puzzle
- Draws a circle and a square
- Matches an object to a picture of that object
- Can count 2–3 objects
- Can say their age
- Identifies common colours such as red, blue, yellow and green
- Can distinguish, match and name colours
- Is interested in similarities and differences
- Is interested in features of animals that make them unique
- Can understand the difference between self and younger children, but not between self and older children

Social and emotional development
- Follows simple directions and accepts suggestions
- Enjoys helping with simple household tasks
- Pays attention for about 3 minutes
- Seeks attention and approval of adults
- Sometimes shows preference for one parent (often the parent of the opposite sex)
- Can make simple choices between two things

- Enjoys making others laugh and being silly
- Enjoys playing alone or near other children
- Spends a lot of time watching and observing
- Will play with other children for a short time, but still does not cooperate or share well
- Enjoys hearing stories about self
- Enjoys playing 'house'
- Enjoys imitating other children and adults
- Will answer whether they are a boy or a girl
- Will show interest in ethnic identities of self and others if exposed to a multicultural setting

Characteristics of being 4

The most appropriate words to describe 4-year-olds are 'energetic' and 'imaginative'. They like to play tag-type games, race around and zip around on their tricycles or scooters. They need to be watched closely as they may over-estimate their abilities and are capable of trying to do some dangerous and crazy tricks. Imagination becomes greater than life for the 4-year-old who often confuses reality and make-believe, resulting in exaggerations and wild stories becoming a common occurrence. They are often silly and impatient and, once they discover humour, put a lot of effort into being silly and telling 'jokes'. Their language may range from silly nonsense words to profanity, accompanied with loud boisterous laughter.

Four-year-olds feel good about the things they can do, show self-confidence and are willing to try new adventures. They have a strong need to feel important and worthwhile. Carers need to praise their accomplishments and provide opportunities for them to experience freedom and independence.

Physical development
- Can use a knife, fork and spoon skilfully
- Needs 10–12 hours of sleep each night
- Can now use the toilet alone
- Dresses self without much assistance (unzip, unbutton and unsnap, but not tie shoes)
- Can feed self, brush teeth, comb hair, wash and dry self, dress, hang up clothes with little assistance
- Walks a straight line
- Hops on one foot
- Pedals and steers a tricycle skilfully
- Jumps over low hurdles
- Runs, jumps, hops and skips around obstacles with ease
- Stacks 10 or more blocks
- Forms shapes and objects out of clay or play dough
- Threads small beads on a string
- Can put together a puzzle of 4–12 pieces

- Catches, bounces and throws a ball easily
- Likes to gallop, turn somersaults, climb ladders and trees; tries to skip

Intellectual development
- Understands the order of daily routines (breakfast before lunch, lunch before dinner, dinner before bed-time)
- Counts 1–7 objects out loud, but not always in the right order
- Understands the concepts of 'tallest, biggest, same, more, on, in, under and above'
- Recognises familiar words in simple books or signs (Stop sign)
- Can recognise some letters if taught and may be able to print own name
- Can place objects in a line from largest to smallest
- Asks a lot of questions, including about birth and death
- Can now speak in fairly complex sentences
- Enjoys singing simple songs, rhymes and nonsense words
- If taught, learns name, address and phone number
- Adapts language to listener's level of understanding
- Asks and answers who, what, when, where and why questions
- Names 6–8 colours and 3 shapes
- Can follow 2 unrelated directions ('Take your shoes off and find your story book.')
- Has a long attention span and finishes activities
- Can continue one activity for 10–15 minutes
- Understands and remembers own accomplishments
- Has basic understanding of concepts related to number, size, weight, colours, textures, distance, position and time
- Understands immediate passage of time as in what happened yesterday; but does not understand calendar time
- May add 'ed' to words: 'I goed to the door and put-ed the cat outside. He hurt-ed me.'

Social and emotional development
- Enjoys playing with other children
- Seeks out adult approval
- Separates from a parent for a short time without crying
- Helps clean up toys at home or school when asked to
- Takes turns and shares (most of the time)
- Understand and obeys simple rules (most of the time)
- Imitates parents of the same sex, particularly in play
- Has a vivid imagination and enjoys pretending often with imaginary playmates
- Loves to tell jokes that may not make any sense at all
- Enjoys dramatic play and role playing
- Changes the rules of a game as it goes along
- Likes to talk and carry on with elaborate conversation
- Capable of feeling jealous
- Persistently asks 'Why?'

- Enjoys showing off and bragging about possessions
- Is fearful of the dark and monsters
- Begins to understand danger and at times can become quite frightened
- Has difficulty separating make-believe from reality
- Lies sometimes to protect self and friends; but does not really understand the concept of lying
- May name-call and tattle freely
- Likes to shock others by using 'forbidden' words
- Can feel intense anger and frustration
- Expresses anger verbally rather than physically (most of the time)
- Will still throw tantrums over minor frustrations

Characteristics of being 5

Five-year-olds are energetic, cheerful and enthusiastic. They like to plan out things and will spend a great deal of time discussing who will do what. They are more sensitive to the feelings of others around them. Best friends become very important. At this age they start kindergarten. (In most states children start kindergarten at age 4 and start all-day school at age 5.) Pace afternoon kindergarten children during the day with a balance of activity and rest. Be sensitive to the needs of all-day kindergarten/school children returning home as they may be tired, hungry, talkative and wanting to share the day's happenings.

Physical development
- Is able to dress self with little assistance
- Learns to skip
- Throws a ball overhead
- Catches bounced balls
- Rides a tricycle skilfully and can ride a bicycle with training wheels
- Balances on either foot for 5–10 seconds
- Cuts on a line with scissors
- Left-or right-hand dominance is established
- Walks down stairs, alternating feet without using a handrail
- Jumps over low objects
- Can run, gallop and tumble, run on tiptoes
- Can jump rope (long rope and short rope)
- Interested in performing tricks like standing on head
- Is capable of learning complex body coordination skills like roller-skating, riding bicycles, striking a ball
- Is able to tie shoelaces
- Uses a knife and fork well
- Can be helpful with small chores
- Sleeps 10–11 hours at night

Intellectual development
- Understands about 13,000 words
- Uses 5–8 words in a sentence

- Likes to argue and reason: 'Because . . .' 'Why?'
- Knows basic colours like red, yellow, blue, green, orange, purple
- Is able to memorise address and phone number
- Understands that stories have a beginning, middle and ending
- Is able to remember stories and repeat them
- Enjoys creating and telling stories
- Understands that books are read from left to right, top to bottom
- Enjoys jokes and riddles
- Draws pictures that represent animals, people and objects
- Enjoys tracing, copying letters and colouring
- Can place objects in order from shortest to tallest
- Can understand and use comparative terms like big, bigger, biggest
- Sorts objects by size
- Identifies some letters of the alphabet and a few numbers
- Understands 'more', 'less' and 'same'; 'before and after'; 'above and below'
- Counts up to 10 objects
- Recognises categories (animals, birds)
- Has good attention span and can concentrate well
- Is project-minded: likes to plan buildings, play scenarios and dramatic play
- Interested in cause and effect
- Can understand time concepts like yesterday, today and tomorrow

Social and emotional development
- Invents games with simple rules
- Organises other children and toys for pretend play
- Still sometimes confuses fantasy with reality
- Often fears loud noises, the dark, animals and some people
- Can take turns and share, but doesn't always want to
- Expresses anger and jealousy physically
- Likes to test muscular strength and motor skills, but is not emotionally ready for competition
- Carries on conversations with other children and adults
- Often excludes other children in play—best friends only
- Uses swear words or 'bathroom words' to get attention
- Can sometimes be very bossy
- Likes to try new things and take risks
- Likes to make own decisions
- Notices when another child is angry or sad—more sensitive to feelings of others
- Prefers company of one or two children at a time
- May become bossy or sulky when others join in
- Likes to feel grown up; boasts about self to younger, less capable children
- Begins to have a very basic understanding of right and wrong
- Plays contentedly and independently with constant supervision

- Understands and respects rules—often asks permission
- Understands and enjoys both giving and receiving
- Enjoys collecting things
- Sometimes needs to get away and be alone
- Can understand relationships among people and similarities and differences in other families
- Seeks adult approval
- Sometimes critical of other children and embarrassed by own mistakes
- Less fearful of the world than toddlers, because understands better
- Has a good sense of humour and enjoys sharing jokes and laughter with adults

Characteristics of being 6–8

This age group tends to settle down to a steadier pace of growing and learning after the first 6 years of life. These young school-age children are more interested now in real life tasks and activities than in pretend and fantasy. School-agers want to make 'real' jewellery, take 'real' photographs and create 'real' collections. Because they have longer attention spans they are more likely to stick with things until the project is finished, the problem solved or the argument resolved. This age group is fascinated by rules and can develop games with extensive rules and rituals, and doing things together with friends, teamwork, and following the rules becomes very important.

It is important for educators and parents to provide opportunities for active play: target throwing, jumping rope, gymnastics, dance and aerobic activities may be of interest. It is also important at this stage to provide opportunities to develop an understanding of the rules by playing simple games, such as cards, dominoes, tic-tac-toe and the like. Equally important is the need to provide opportunities for children to do non-competitive team activities, such as working together on a jigsaw puzzle or planting a garden. Encourage children's sense of accomplishment by providing opportunities to build models, cook or bake, make crafts, practise music or work with wood. Encourage creating collections and special boxes to store the collections. Encourage reading and writing by creating opportunities to produce stories with scripts; create music for plays and puppet shows; record events; conduct experiments; produce a newspaper. Take children on field trips to museums, workplaces and other neighbourhoods.

Physical development
- Enjoys testing muscle strength and skills
- May have a growth spurt that gives them a gawky awkward appearance
- Can catch small balls

- Can tie shoelaces
- Skilled at using scissors and small tools
- Demonstrates a good sense of balance
- Enjoys copying designs and shapes, letters and numbers
- Can print name
- Develops permanent teeth

Intellectual development
- Enjoys creating special collections
- Is able to learn difference between left and right
- Can begin to understand time and the days of the week
- Increased speaking and listening vocabularies—doubled
- Has a longer attention span
- Increased ability to problem-solve
- Enjoys planning and building
- Takes a keen interest in reading
- Interested in magic and tricks
- May reverse printed letters (such as 'b/d')

Social and emotional development
- Being with friends becomes increasingly important
- Interested in rules and rituals
- May have a best friend and an enemy
- Shows a strong desire to perform well, do things the right way
- Girls want to play more with girls; boys with boys
- Does not handle well criticism or failure
- Generally enjoys caring for and playing with younger children
- Seeks a sense of security in groups, organised play and clubs
- Begins to see things from another child's point of view, but still very self-centred
- May become upset when behaviour or school work is ignored
- Views things as black or white, right or wrong, wonderful or terrible, with very little middle ground

Characteristics of being 9–12

Children at this age are developing a sense of self. They have an increasing need to gain social acceptance and experience achievement. Friends become increasingly important. Close friends are usually of the same sex, although children in this age group are becoming increasingly more interested in peers of the opposite sex. They develop secret codes or passwords and their own language or word meanings, sometimes with well-thought-out rituals—all for the purpose of friendship bonding.

They tend to think that they do not need any adult care or supervision and may test your patience in this area. Yet, left to care for themselves, they can become unhappy, lonely and even frightened.

Provide opportunities for older school-agers to help out with real skills: cooking, sewing, building something, putting up a tent and so forth. Provide time and space for them to be alone where they can read, daydream or do school work uninterrupted. Encourage children to participate in an organised club or youth group. Encourage older children to help out with younger children under your supervision, but avoid burdening them with too many adult responsibilities. Allow time for play and relaxation. Provide opportunities for older children to play games of strategy: draughts, chess, dominoes and Monopoly® are popular with this age group. Older children have larger appetites than younger children and will need to eat more, so have plenty of healthy nutritious food available for them.

Physical development
- Girls are generally as much as 2 years ahead of boys in physical maturity
- Girls may begin to menstruate at 10 years of age
- Shows improvement in coordination and reaction time
- Shows increase in body strength and hand dexterity

Intellectual development
- Interested in reading fictional stories, magazines and project books
- May develop special interest in hobbies or collections
- Likes to fantasise and daydream about the future
- May take a keen interest in discussing a future career
- Can understand concepts without having direct hands-on experience

Social and emotional development
- Enjoys being a member of a club or group
- Likes to make up secret codes, languages, rituals and rules
- Increased interest in competitive sports
- Can control their anger or outbursts more
- May belittle or defy adult authority
- Begins to see parents and authority figures as fallible human beings

The main source of information for this section came from the National Network for Child Care, Oesterreich, L., Holt, B., and Karas, S., *Iowa Family Child Care Handbook*, 1995, Iowa State University Extension, Ames, IA.

Understanding fitness and its importance

What is fitness and what are its benefits?

Fitness is defined as a health-base in which an individual has sufficient energy to enjoy life and avoid fatigue, and to meet with unforeseen emergencies.

Research evidence indicates that physical activity brings health benefits for children, including:
• improving aerobic endurance
• making the heart pump more strongly
• strengthening bones and muscles
• reducing the risk of heart disease
• helping to lower blood pressure and resting heart rate
• providing more energy for play, school work, daily chores
• helping to maintain healthy body weight
• reducing stress.

We need to reinforce the values of exercise in an age-appropriate way to our children. It is not just the 'doing' of the exercise or activity, but the development of a 'knowing' attitude that is so important. Children need to realise that you cannot 'store' fitness like you can store food in a fridge or money in a bank. Fitness/activity must be a regular occurrence—ideally daily! You need to observe children at play and take a 'mental snapshot' of their activity level. Are they generally active throughout the activity session? Do they show through body language (such as facial expressions) enjoyment of what they are doing? Do they express verbally their excitement and 'fun' in what they are doing?

What is the F.I.T.T. principle?

The **F.I.T.T. Principle**
     F—Frequency
     I—Intensity
     T—Time
     T—Type
states that we need to engage at least 3 times per week in ongoing, continuous activity of at least 20–30 minutes duration, in our target heart range. A variety of activities—such as walking, jogging, swimming and water exercises, cycling, dancing, roller-blading, sporting activities (basketball, tennis, soccer, netball), rope jumping, cross-country skiing, hiking, gardening, canoeing—is

recommended, rather than just one type of activity, so that different muscle groups are used and not over-used.

Educators of young children, physical educators and parents need to realise that in teaching children to be effective and efficient movers several, if not all, of the health- and skill-related components are involved in generating a successful outcome. For example, to run efficiently involves coordination and balance, cardiovascular and muscular endurance; to dodge involves these components, but also agility, spurts of speed and alertness/reaction. A specific technique is involved in developing an overhand throw; but equally important is to develop good arm, wrist and finger strength to execute it.

Large muscle groups should be warmed up through low–to moderate gentle and rhythmical activity first, before gradually increasing the intensity. Stretching should be smooth and rhythmical, through the full range of motion of 'warmed' large group muscles. Muscles should never be stretched 'cold' or with ballistic movements; hyper-extending any joint areas should be avoided. Emphasise the importance of maintaining good posture or form while doing the exercise. Proper breathing needs to be taught—when to exhale; when to inhale. The physical educator should teach *total* fitness, involving both health- and skill-related aspects, in a safe, clean and appropriate learning environment.

How much activity is enough?

Moderate activity is valuable and beneficial. Active children become active adults. Any activity is better than no activity. Experts recommend that primary school-age children accumulate at least 30–60 minutes of age and developmentally appropriate physical activity—daily! More than 30–60 minutes should be encouraged and extended periods of inactivity for children discouraged! Parents need to monitor the time children spend watching TV, playing computer games and other very passive activities.

Keep fitness inherent throughout the Physical Education lesson rather than teaching it as a training regime. Exposure to a variety of interesting, enjoyable and beneficial activities at the developmentally appropriate age level is highly recommended!

Make fitness fun! Children are not mini-adults! They simply obtain their fitness by doing activities that they enjoy. Imposing 'training' on them will only create a battle of resistance. Developing a love for being active at an early age should carry over into developing a healthy, fit lifestyle as an adult. It is the 'process' of exercising on a regular basis, so that it becomes a habitual and a permanent part of one's lifestyle, that is important; the product, fitness, will follow!

Fitness is for everyone, regardless of gender, culture or ethnicity, physical competence and disabilities. The true 'mission' for educators is to help children from an early age to enjoy and learn about the benefits of physical activity, so that they will develop personal habits of doing exercise regularly and thus continue to be active for the rest of their lives.

The health-related components of fitness

The health-related components of fitness are:
1. Cardiovascular fitness
2. Flexibility
3. Muscular strength
4. Muscular endurance

Cardiovascular fitness

Cardiovascular (CV) fitness has to do with the efficient working of the heart–lung system to supply fuel, oxygen, to the working muscles. CV fitness requires a strong heart muscle.

The heart muscle becomes stronger through exercise, just like other muscles of the body. It is important that the heart be exercised regularly from an early age; otherwise, it will never work as efficiently as it should. A strong healthy heart, that increases in size and power, can pump more blood with each beat and, therefore, the heart rate will be lower for any given amount of work, as well as at rest. This tells us that our heart is not working as strenuously as an unfit heart.

Heart rate (pulse) is important to determine if a person is doing enough exercise (intensity). The average resting heart rate of a child is about 80 beats per minute; of an adult, 70–80 beats per minute; but a trained athlete's heart rate can be in the low 50s!

Aerobic exercise is activity for which the body can supply adequate oxygen to the working muscles to sustain activity for a long time. This produces CV fitness. Regular exercise reduces the risk of heart disease by building CV fitness, burning off kilojoules/calories to help control body fat and developing muscular endurance.

Cardiovascular activities

THE HEART WORKOUT

Have children move in different ways to your signals: walk, power walk, walk with quick changes of direction; walk on toes, walk on heels; walk backwards; march, march, changing direction every 4 steps; jog straight ahead, jog with quick changes of direction; skip happily along; slide-step keeping low and moving in different directions.

On the signal 'Freeze!' have children put one hand against their chest (left-hand side) and feel their heart beat. Let the other hand open and close to show the pulse beat that they feel.

PULSE BEAT

Have children 'listen' to their hearts beating by placing 'pointer' and 'tall person' fingers (2nd and 3rd fingers) on either side of the Adam's apple (carotid artery) and count the number of beats in 30 seconds. Multiply by 2 to get the beats per minute (b.p.m.).

Or place 2nd and 3rd fingers just above the base of the thumb on the wrist to locate the radial artery.

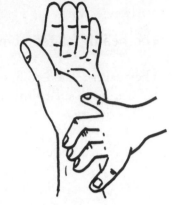

Flexibility

Flexibility is the range of motion around a joint. It is how we 'stretch'. Stretching is one of the most important, yet most neglected, fitness activities that should be done almost every day of one's life. Research has clearly indicated that children need to experience stretching activities on a daily basis and from an early age. Often this is not the present case. Most young children are flexible, but they quickly lose this ability if they do not stretch regularly. Developing good flexibility can help prevent injury, help prevent muscle strain, muscle spasms and soreness and backache; keep muscles toned, improve spinal mobility and maintain joint suppleness.

As children grow older their flexibility increases until adolescence, then they can become progressively less flexible. Generally, girls tend to be more flexible than boys. Some children have a high degree of flexibility. We say that they are 'double-jointed', but correctly their unusual flexibility is a genetic trait that makes their joints 'hyper-mobile'.

Research suggests that muscles need to be stretched to about 10% beyond their normal length to bring about improved flexibility. The result of a joint not being moved regularly through its full range of motion is a shortening of muscles and ligaments. Lack of use, injury (body part immobilised by a cast), poor posture and poor working posture, can result in loss of flexibility in a fairly short time. Thus stretching for flexibility needs to be a daily occurrence!

The benefits of stretching include:
• an increased range of motion of joints
• improved flexibility of muscles and joints
• improved coordination and overall body management (including posture)

• prevention of injuries, such as muscle strains and pulls, muscle spasms and soreness, shin splints, backaches
• development of overall body awareness
• generally an improved kinaesthetic sense.

Remember these precautions as well:
• Never stretch 'cold' muscles.
• Always 'warm up' children first with low–moderate activity. Movements should be gentle and rhythmical, then gradually increased in intensity.
• Try to use all the major muscle groups in the warm-up activity.
• When performing an aerobic activity, have children stretch before and after.
• Avoid ballistic-type stretching—use slow gentle stretching, through the whole range of motion, or hold static stretches for at least 10 seconds.
• Avoid exercises that hyper-extend any joint areas.
• Don't stretch a muscle until it becomes painful: pain is no gain!
• Don't overstretch weak muscles.
• Don't stretch any swollen joints.
• No massive weight-bearing exercises should be used. Children can use their own body weight to develop strength.

Many flexibility exercises have also been included in the Kids with Zip sessions. We encourage you to do these stretches along with your children. You need to know, however, that there are some ways of stretching that should be avoided. Some of the exercises we did as children are no longer recognised as suitable. In fact some are now considered dangerous. The following Stretching Do's and Don'ts provide reasons why particular types of stretch should be excluded and suggest alternatives. Photocopy the information and keep it nearby when you are doing your Fit Sessions!

STRETCHING DO'S AND DON'TS

Name of exercise	Why exclude?	Alternative
1. Side bends—standing and seated	Bad for the middle and lower back.	Lying on your back with arms above head. Bend gently to side.
2. Straight leg toe touch—standing and seated	Can tear the muscles at the back of the upper leg and lower muscles.	Sit on floor with legs straight and arms supporting behind. Place both hands on outstretched leg and slowly and gently slide your hands up your leg until you feel a slight stretch. Hold for 5 secs. Repeat 5 times.

3. Hurdle stretch	Strains the ligaments of the knee that is bent.	Lying on your back with legs straight. Pull knees slowly and gently up to chest with hands. Hold for 5 secs.
4. Alternate toe touch	May cause lower back damage especially if not fit.	From seated position with legs bent. Keeping back straight alternately touch hand to toes of opposite leg.
5. Straight leg sit-ups	Bad for lower back Does not strengthen stomach muscles sufficiently.	Bent leg sit-ups with arms folded across chest. Keep back straight. Need not come all the way up.
6. Leg raises— holding legs off ground	Can cause too much pressure on the discs. Is not a good stomach firming exercise.	Lying on back with knees bent and arms to the side. Slowly and gently bring both knees up until kneecaps point straight to sky.
7. Push-ups that sag	Can cause too much pressure on discs in back. Ineffective for improving upper body strength.	Start with half push-up from kneeling position with knees straight under seat. As strength improves move knees further back until a full push-up position is achieved. Remember no sag.
8. Banana bends lying on stomach holding ankles and pulling them up towards head	Hyper-extension of the back.	Lie on stomach with hands under chin and legs stretched and together. Slowly and gently raise one leg at a time to a point where a slight stretch is felt. Hold for 5 secs.
9. Over the head toes to touch ground	Can cause damage to neck.	In standing position hold your hand against side of head. Push against hand slowly, hand giving resistance. Repeat with hand on forehead.
10. Star jumps	Stress on all joints.	Walk!

Stretching activities

Children with movement difficulties need to be taught to stretch from an early age, as they are more injury- and accident-prone. Teaching young children how to fall safely or recover from a falling position has a strong carry-over value for the rest of their lives. We have presented several different, interesting and fun ways of getting kids to stretch and keep stretching. In fact we suggest that you do these yourself on a daily basis!

1. GOOD MORNING, WAKEY-WAKEY STRETCH

Pretend that you are still in your bed and just beginning to wake up. Lying on your back, stretch as wide as possible. Do this slowly. Stretch like a pencil. Yawn!
Smile a 'good morning' smile! ☺

WIDE STRETCH   PENCIL STRETCH

- Now in your own space stretch your arms up to the sky.
- Raise up on your toes as you stretch upwards.
- Let your eyes follow your hands.
- Circle your arms in towards the middle making large circles from the middle.
- Gently turn from side to side, pushing the hand out to the opposite side.
- Shake all over like a wet dog coming out of the water.
- Slowly sink to the floor into back-lying position.
- Raise one leg, holding it at the ankle with both hands; keep it straight and gently press it towards your head. Repeat with the other leg.
- In back-lying position, do a 'pencil' stretch extending arms overhead and hold for 10 seconds.
- Do 'Angels in the snow' (see page 73), then another 'pencil' stretch.

ARM CIRCLES   WET DOG

LEG STRETCH

2. NODDING HEADS

Stand tall. Gently and slowly nod your head as if you are saying 'Yes!' Now gently shake your head as if you are saying 'No!'

3. SHRUGS!

Stand tall. Shrug your shoulders as if you are saying 'I don't know!'

4. ROLLS

Gently roll your shoulders backwards, then forwards.

5. SKY REACHES

Stand tall. Stretch one arm up towards the sky, then stretch the other arm. Continue.

NODDING HEADS   SHRUGS

ROLLS

SKY REACHES

PROPELLERS

6. PROPELLERS

Gently circle arms forwards.

7. WINGERS!

Start with arms bent and parallel to ground, hands at chest level and closed. Gently pull arms backwards, squeezing shoulder blades together and continue to open sideways holding the stretch. Repeat from beginning.

WINGERS

BELLY–BUTTON CIRCLES

8. BELLY-BUTTON CIRCLES

Pretend that your belly-button is the centre of the circle. Trace 3 circles in one direction, then 3 circles in the opposite direction. Repeat.

9. SIDE STRETCHER

Standing tall, slowly reach down one side of your body, 'walking' your fingers as far down as you can go. Walk your fingers back up to starting position, and then walk your fingers down the other side.

SIDE STRETCHER

10. PERISCOPE!

To start, lie on your back, arms at your sides and legs straight. Bring one leg straight upwards and grasp the ankle with your hands. Gently press it towards you for 10 seconds, then repeat with the other leg.

PERISCOPE

FINGER STRETCHER

11. FINGER STRETCHER

In stand tall position, interlock your fingers of both hands, then gently straighten your arms pushing the palms of your hands outwards. Hold this stretch for 5–10 seconds; relax. Now stretch in this position with arms overhead and gently close and open your hands for 10 seconds.

12. BUTTERFLY STRETCH

In sitting position, place the bottoms of your feet together. Holding at the ankles with your hands, let your arms gently push along the inside of knees. Hold for 10 seconds.

BUTTERFLY STRETCH

13. FOOT ARTIST

In sitting position, lean back on hands for support. Lift one leg and draw circles in the air with your pointed toes. Now draw circles in the opposite direction. Repeat using the other foot. Use your foot to trace your favourite letter and favourite number.

FOOT ARTIST

14. CALF STRETCH

Stand facing a wall with hands flat against wall for support. Point both feet to wall. Keep the front leg bent and the back leg straight, pressing the heel of the back foot to the floor. Reverse leg positions and repeat.

CALF STRETCH

15. SPRINTER STRETCH

Begin in all-fours position. Move one leg forwards until the knee of this front leg is directly over the ankle. Extend the other leg back.

SPRINTER STRETCH

16. QUAD STRETCH

In stand tall position with hand support on nearby wall, bend one leg gently back until heel of foot is touching back of upper leg. Hold for 10 seconds. Repeat with other leg.

QUAD STRETCH

Muscular strength

Muscular strength is measured by the amount of force you can exert with a single maximum effort. Good muscular strength helps to increase work effort, to decrease the chance of injury, to prevent back injury and poor posture, to improve athletic performance and, perhaps, even to save a life. Through improving your child's muscular strength, the strength of bones, tendons and ligaments is also increased. Children whose bones are still growing need to have low-impact exercises—otherwise the result could be permanent growth-stunting damage to the growth plates.

Discuss with children the importance of having strong arm muscles to carry out daily work and play, such as taking out the garbage, bringing in the groceries, raking the lawn, chopping wood, throwing a football, swinging a baseball bat, hanging and swinging on playground apparatus, swimming and meeting unforeseen emergencies.

Strengthening activities

1. ANIMAL WALKS

Begin in your home space. Show me how you can move like the following animals:

Crab—walk on all fours face upwards.

Kangaroo—jumping, with hands held up in front.

Puppy dog—walk on all fours.

KANGAROO

Bunny hop—on all fours, with hands moving forwards first, then feet. Continue in this way.

BUNNY HOP

Seal—move along using your forearms and dragging your feet behind you as you move along.

SEAL WALK

Inchworm—from front support position, walk your feet up to your hands, then walk your hands away from your feet. Keep repeating this pattern as you 'inchworm' along the floor.

BUCKING BRONCO

INCHWORM

Bucking bronco—take your weight on your hands and kick your legs gently up into the air. How high can your legs go?

Crab walk greeting—greet your child on all fours, face upwards, by lifting one foot upwards and shaking your child's foot. Repeat shaking with the other foot.

CRAB WALK GREETING

Lame puppy dog—on all fours, hands and feet, walk like a puppy dog who has an injured back foot.

Animal walk—make up your own animal walk!

2. ANKLE TAPS

Begin in hook-lying position (see page 71). Curl up to tap inside of your ankle with opposite foot. Return to hook-lying and repeat with other hand and ankle.

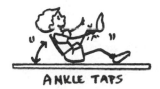

3. SEAT WADDLES

In long-sit position (see page 70), move yourself forwards and backwards by using only your seat muscles.

4. HAND WALK

In front support position (see page 71), walk your hands 4 steps in front, walk hands 4 steps back; walk hands to the right side, to the left side. Repeat.

5. CLOCK WALK

In front support position, keep your feet in the centre of the 'clock' and walk your hands to 3 o'clock, 9 o'clock, 12 o'clock and so on.

6. FIRE HYDRANTS

In all fours position, with hips square and right knee bent, raise right leg to side and lower it again. Repeat 8 times. Change legs and repeat another 8 times.

7. THIGH LIFTERS

Begin in half-hook/half-long-sit position (see page 70). Raise and lower your extended leg 8 times, alternately pointing (away) and flexing (pointing toes towards) your foot. Reverse leg positions and repeat.

8. ANKLE BUILDERS

In hook-sit position (see page 70), start with one leg and point your foot away from you, flex your foot by pointing toes towards you, circle it one way, circle it the other way. Repeat with the ankle of the other foot.

Muscular endurance

Muscular endurance has to do with muscles' ability to continue to contract over a long period. Good muscular endurance gives you

the ability to repeat a movement without getting tired or to hold a position or carry something for a long period of time without being fatigued. Children with good muscular endurance will enjoy and have greater success in their daily work activities, in play, and in sporting and athletic competitions.

Muscular endurance activities
'Spotting' means to move alongside with the children as they perform the activity or task, helping them if necessary but, more importantly, keeping alert to support them if they slip or lose their grip. Spotting is necessary for activities 1–4 below.

1. Hand walk across the high bar.

2. Travel across the high horizontal ladder using hands and feet.

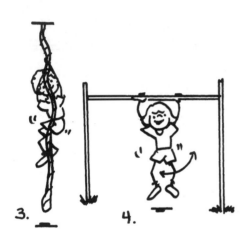

3. Climb up a hanging rope, hand over hand; and hand under hand to go down. Remember not to slide down the rope to avoid rope burn!

4. On the high bar hang by your knees upside down and swing.

5. When a TV commercial comes on, do curl-ups. Get into hook-lying position, cross hands on shoulders. Curl up until shoulders are off the floor, then slowly roll down to starting position. Repeat.

6. Lean your back against the wall, bending legs at right angles and hold this position for 10 seconds, 20 seconds, 30 seconds.

7. Rope-jump on the spot.

Skill-related components of fitness

Agility, balance, coordination, power, speed and reaction are considered to be the main components of skill-related physical fitness.

1. **AGILITY** is the ability to quickly and accurately change direction of your body movement in general space. Examples are downhill skiing and wrestling.

2. **BALANCE** is the ability to maintain body equilibrium while on the spot or while moving; examples would be moving on a balance beam, water skiing, board surfing, snow boarding.

3. **COORDINATION** is the ability to control body part movements to perform motor tasks well and accurately, such as juggling, baseball batting, hitting a golf ball, kicking a ball, striking a ball with a racquet.

4. **POWER** is the ability to quickly transfer energy into force, such as putting the shot, throwing a javelin. Power is a combination of strength and speed and is both health- and skill-related.

5. **SPEED** is the ability to perform a movement quickly, such as running the 100 m/yard sprint.

6. **REACTION** (your alertness level) is the ability to respond quickly to a stimulation, such as starting a sprint race or being a racing car driver.

Part 2 provides many ideas for developing and enhancing these skill-related components of fitness, as well as the health-related components.

Healthy lifestyle habits/skills checklist

Tick the lifestyle habits or skills that you do each day.
- ❏ Eat a nutritious breakfast almost every morning.
- ❏ Brush my teeth after each meal (including my tongue).
- ❏ Floss my teeth once a day.
- ❏ Drink at least 4–6 glasses of water each day.
- ❏ Eat at least 4–6 different vegetables each day.
- ❏ Eat 2–3 different fruits each day.
- ❏ Drink 2–3 glasses of milk each day.
- ❏ Watch carefully the amount of junk food (high fats, sugar, cakes, chocolates, potato crisps) eaten in a week.
- ❏ Watch TV no more than 1–2 hours a day.
- ❏ Do regular aerobic activity at least 3 times a week and at least 30 minutes' duration of continuous activity.
- ❏ Warm up properly before doing any moderate to strenuous activity.

- ❏ Do stretching exercises each day for about 10–15 minutes.
- ❏ Do strengthening exercises each day for about 15 minutes.
- ❏ Try to get at least 6–8 hours of sleep each night.
- ❏ Try to relax for at least 15 minutes at some point in my day.
- ❏ Try to keep good posture (when sitting, standing still or moving).
- ❏ Do activity on a regular basis, at least 3 times per week.
- ❏ Strive for good time management, but make it flexible and adaptable.
- ❏ Try to read the newspaper or a book each day.
- ❏ Take up a hobby that I will enjoy, such as playing a musical instrument.
- ❏ Have a medical check-up on a regular basis (once a year).
- ❏ Have my teeth checked and cleaned at least once a year.
- ❏ Try to do a kind deed each day.
- ❏ Remember to smile often and be considerate of others. ☺
- ❏ Try to minimise stress in my life!

10 strategies to encourage reluctant children

1. Observe them. *Why* are they reluctant? Because they are overweight, have poor coordination, feel unsafe, fear of failure, insecure, low self-esteem.
2. Create a safe, fun, positive environment. Ensure that there is absolutely no physical threat, no ridicule, no bullying, no put-downs. No 'emotional hurts'.
3. Provide feedback that is instantaneous—at the 'time of doing'. Give praise and encouragement; words such as: 'I really liked the way you did that.' 'I'm so proud of you! You ran all the way!'
4. Ensure that they experience success within a short time.
5. May need to offer some kind of incentive or reward. Instant reward is praise and encouragement. Reward could follow a goal: 'After we go cycling together, we will go to the movies.'
6. Keep within the limits of the children's abilities. Don't force them or constantly be at them. Ideally, we would like each child to take responsibility for their own activity.
7. Don't be over-protective.
8. Don't confuse children's needs with their wants. Young children do not have the experience or knowledge to know what is good for them. For example, the child who consistently says to the parent, 'I don't want to go outside to play, I would rather watch TV.' is expressing a 'want', not a 'need'. In this situation, as a caring adult we need to impose our knowledge of the importance of exercise on the child and encourage, and even insist, that they do go out to play regularly.
9. Establish firmness and consistency. Insist that you will do an activity together and stick to this.
10. Vary the activities that you do with your children to sustain their interest.

Understanding nutrition and its importance

The importance of maintaining good nutrition from birth onwards cannot be emphasised enough! Children today are strongly influenced by what they see and hear on TV. They do not distinguish between entertainment, advertising and factual information. They can get so hooked into the advertising that they literally demand a certain product (such as the heavily sugared products that are so predominant in advertising directed towards children) and refuse to eat anything else. Another growing concern is the nutritional effect of frequently eating out at popular fast-food restaurants. Research indicates that the most popular vegetable consumed in large quantities by children is the french fry and that the lack of fibre in a child's diet could result in severe constipation. Most schools operating a canteen at recess break and lunch break are now offering a much healthier selection of foods and drinks. Parents need to ensure that they make a nutritious school lunch pack for their children and that the children are getting plenty of water to drink.

The nutrition pyramid

Good health comes from a healthy lifestyle that translates to regular exercise, as well as a healthy diet. The saying 'We are what we eat' has a lot of truth.

So, what is healthy eating?

The nutrition pyramid offers a general daily guideline to follow for maintaining a healthy balanced diet. The base of the pyramid consists of the cereal, bread, rice and pasta group; followed by the fruit group (2–3 servings) and vegetable group (3–5 servings). The next level is the dairy products groups, including milk, yoghurt and cheese (2 servings). Calcium content of dairy foods is important, especially for women. Parallel to the dairy products group is the poultry, meat, fish, eggs and nuts group, and 2–3 servings is generally the recommended level. Iron from red meat is important for maintaining healthy blood cells. The top level of the nutrition pyramid contains the fats, oils and sugar. Children need to be monitored so that they consume only small quantities of these foods. It is better to snack from the lower food groups and leave those foods at the top for special treats or part of a bigger meal.

How much should you be serving your child? Nutritional experts recommend that children should have a daily intake of around 2000–2200 calories made up of approximately 8–9 servings from the complex carbohydrates group, 3 servings of fruit, 4 servings of vegetables (use different colours), 3 dairy servings and about 180g of meat serving. The number and size of servings may vary according to the age, size and activity of the child; but it is important that the child receives the equivalent of 2 cups of milk a day and drinks about 4 glasses of water.

A serving is approximately:

½ cup of complex carbohydrates, 1 slice of bread
1 cup of green leaf vegetables, ½ cup of other vegetables
1 piece of fruit
1 cup of milk/yoghurt, 60g cheese
90g of meat product, 1 egg
2 tablespoons of nuts

A look at the nutrition pyramid below provides the key food groups from which to select and a recommendation of the number of servings from each of these groups per day.

Nutrition pyramid

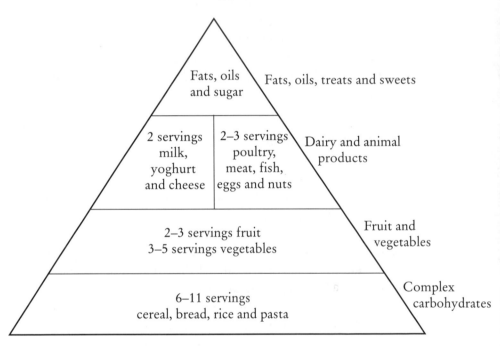

Food groups

COMPLEX CARBOHYDRATES at the base of the pyramid provide us with B-vitamins, minerals and fibre. Importantly, they are low in fats and kilojoules/calories.

Wholegrain products, rather than processed products, are preferable as they are a higher source of vitamins, minerals and fibre.

FRUIT AND VEGETABLES are in the middle level of the pyramid and are an excellent source of vitamins (especially vitamins A and C) and minerals.

DAIRY AND ANIMAL PRODUCTS are at the next level of the pyramid and these foods provide us with calcium for bones, protein, iron and zinc. Some of these dairy and animal products contain high levels of cholesterol and, consequently, need monitoring.

FATS AND OILS AS WELL AS TREATS AND SWEETS should be used and eaten sparingly. Avoid saturated fats; instead, use unsaturated fats such as olive oil.

Tips for encouraging healthy eating in children

We all have our likes and dislikes with regard to food. It is important, however, that parents encourage, support and provide a healthy lifestyle for their children. There is a large amount of detailed information on nutrition (including health recipe ideas) in books, magazines and on the Internet. Following are suggestions that may be the springboard to ensuring that your children and, indeed, the whole family have a healthy diet. Additional ideas to promote a healthy lifestyle are discussed in the section on overweight children.

Tips

- Involve children in the shopping, planning and preparation of healthy meals wherever possible.
- There is a saying that we eat with our eyes before we eat with our mouth. The visual presentation of food is extremely important, especially for children. The food needs to be presented in a simple, but interesting way. It is a good idea to use contrasts of colour, shape and texture whenever possible in your presentation. For example, make a face from mashed potatoes, baby carrots and peas.
- Start the day with breakfast! Eating a nutritious breakfast kick-starts the brain, improves physical and mental performance, helps to maintain healthy weight and fuels your 'empty tank' to get you going for the day, through the day.
- Eat more 'live' foods than processed foods. Eat 2–3 servings of fruit, such as apples, oranges, bananas, peaches, pears and grapes and 3–5 vegetable servings, such as carrots, celery, corn on the cob, peas in the pod, capsicums. Cut down on processed foods, such as potato crisps and corn chips, cakes and chocolate.
- Eat regular meals. In fact try 'grazing' through the day, eating 5–6 smaller but nutritious lighter meals. This can keep your metabolism operating more efficiently. Don't skip meals—this can lead to binge eating or over-eating and often to eating foods that have little if any nutritional value.
- Cut down on foods that are high in salt, sugar and fats. Just eat them occasionally as little 'treats'.
- Choose leaner meats, low-fat dairy products and foods that are prepared with little or no fat, not fried.
- You may need to be patient and persistent to get some children to eat healthy foods, but in the long run it will be worth the effort.
- Snacks between meals can be part of a healthy diet for children as long as they include foods such as fruit, yoghurt and reduced fat products, and not items such as sweets, crisps and chocolate.

- Avoid diets that restrict food intake for children. Do not restrict their kilojoule/calorie intake unless recommended by a doctor.
- Variety from all the food groups is essential for children to gain the necessary vitamins, minerals and fibre from their diet.
- Make available a variety of fresh fruit and vegetables which are both simple to prepare as well as nutritious.
- Eat snacks wisely. Choose food that is high in carbohydrates and nutrients that are best at sustaining energy. Snacks are a good way to refuel when your blood sugar level is feeling low.
- Try to balance the foods you eat each day so that you are eating from each of the food groups.
- Moderation is the key. It is not necessary to eliminate all sweets and treats, but they do need to be given in moderation. Overuse of even healthy foods, for example, vegetables, especially at the expense of other food groups is also not recommended. The key is in maintaining a balanced nutritious diet.
- Be aware of your child's weaknesses. Don't have foods such as sweets or crisps that tempt your children lying around. Replace these foods with fruit in a bowl or raw vegetables, such as carrots, and encourage the children to eat them.
- Regular meals throughout the day are important. Whenever possible, family meals at the table should occur with parents modelling healthy eating habits.
- Smaller meals taken more frequently are a preferred method of eating throughout the day. Eating 5 smaller meals is healthier than our traditional 3 large meals.
- Emphasis on complex carbohydrates that are high in vitamins, minerals and fibre need to be promoted in daily meals.
- Drink plenty of water—up to 6–8 glasses (1–2 litres) a day. Drink more water when exercising or when it is very hot.
- Keep your weight at a healthy level by balancing nutritious eating with regular exercise. Input = Output.

Make a commitment to encourage and support healthy nutritional eating and regular sustainable exercise for your family. Go on, go for it—you might be surprised just how good *you* feel!

Tips for helping overweight children

Children may be overweight due to a number of factors

GENETIC
The genetic link increases the likelihood of obesity in children. It does not, however, necessarily mean that a child who has a family history of obesity will be overweight.

UNHEALTHY EATING HABITS
If a child's eating habits include a high intake of fat and kilojoules/calories and eating between meals then it is quite possible, if combined with low levels of activity, for this to lead to obesity.

INACTIVITY

Simply put, if a child's kilojoule/calorie intake exceeds the output then weight will be gained.

The activity level of the child is an important determining factor in this equation. Children need to be encouraged to be active and limit excessive periods of sedentary activities, such as watching TV and playing computer games. This may mean that we as adults need to take a leading role in this lifestyle.

MEDICAL REASONS

In rare cases, endocrine disorders can cause obesity.

Tips

- Assisting an overweight child quite often commences with viewing the family lifestyle. The nutritional and physical activity habits of the family need to reflect and promote a healthy lifestyle that they will be able to maintain. This means that sudden and complete lifestyle alterations, such as crash diets and excessive exercise regimes, are not a long-term solution for adults or children. In the previous section some suggestions are given to encourage healthy eating in children. These all apply to children who are overweight and some of the more relevant ideas are repeated here with some additional suggestions.
- Be sensitive to your child's weight problems and let them know that no matter what their weight they are still loved and accepted.
- Support your child. Encourage them to talk about their weight and how they feel, if at all possible.
- Increase your family's physical activity. This may need to be a gradual process for all concerned.
- Unless it has been medically recommended, do not place your child on a diet that restricts the amount eaten.
- Teach your child the difference between hunger and craving. They will be hungry when their stomach feels empty and if they have this feeling offer them a healthy snack or a drink of water. A craving is a want not a need: I see it or think about it, so I want it. Don't give in to their cravings.
- Teach healthy eating habits and follow the recommendations of the nutrition pyramid.
- Parents should be healthy role models when it comes to nutrition.
- Involve the children in shopping for, planning and preparing healthy meals wherever possible.
- Use reduced fat products wherever possible.
- Present healthy food in interesting ways (see section above).
- Balance high fat foods with low fat foods.
- Use substitutes such as margarine instead of butter; yoghurt instead of ice-cream.
- Use low-fat methods of cooking food. For example, grill rather than fry.
- Use lean meats instead of high fat meats in food such as hamburgers.

- Take the skin off chicken.
- Offer fish as often as possible.
- Keep between-meal snacks light and healthy.
- The changes in your child's diet have to be gradual. Large sudden changes may be met with a lot of resistance from the child.
- Moderate sweets rather than eliminate them.
- Eat as a family wherever possible and make the atmosphere pleasant so that the children associate healthy eating with pleasant times.
- With any change there are likely to be obstacles and setbacks. Your patience and persistence may be tested to get some children to eat healthy foods, but eventually this will pay off. Strive to make nutritional eating more appealing and easier to stick to. The result should be a happier healthier child! It has to be worth the effort.

Understanding motor fitness and its importance

Gross-motor coordination

Gross-motor movements are fundamental movement skills (FMS) that involve large muscle groups and different body parts, such as feet, legs, trunk, head, arms and hands. FMS are the foundation movement for more complex and specialised skills required to play low-organised games, sports, gymnastics, dance and recreational activities. The gross-motor skills can be categorised into 3 main skill areas.

BODY MANAGEMENT SKILLS which involve controlling body balance whether on the move (dynamic balance), such as starting and stopping, rolling, landing and falling, turning, twisting, bending, swinging, stretching and dodging; or while stationary (static balance), such as balancing on one foot. Body management skills also include awareness of body parts and how the body moves in personal and general space.

LOCOMOTION SKILLS which include walking, running, dodging, jumping and landing, hopping, leaping, skipping and sliding. Locomotion skills need to be learned from an early age.

OBJECT CONTROL SKILLS which include hand–eye and/or foot–eye coordination in manipulating such objects as balls, hoops, jump ropes, racquets, bats and hockey sticks. These skills include rolling, underhand throwing, overhand throwing, catching, bouncing, dribbling, striking skills with one or both hands, and kicking and trapping skills.

Current research suggests that if children do not reach a degree of competence and confidence in FMS by the sixth grade (ages 11–12), they will not pursue regular activity as an adult!

Fine-motor coordination

Fine-motor coordination involves the ability to control the small muscles of the body and is usually defined as the ability to coordinate the action of the eyes and hands together in performing precise manipulative movements (eye–hand coordination). The early forerunners of fine-motor control appear to be the reflex grasp and avoidance reactions that become integrated and refined with increasing age and experience.

Most manipulative activities require the use of the two hands working together to perform the task. Opening a door is a single-handed manipulative task, while drawing and handwriting are graphic activities—a third type of manipulative activity.

In general, children show the most improvement in simple fine-motor control behaviours from 4–6 years; whereas more complex control behaviours tend to improve gradually from 5–12 years. Isolated finger, hand, wrist and foot movements tend to improve significantly from 5–8 years.

Vision is known to play an important role in fine-motor control. Continued visual experience is necessary for feedback and refinement of early guided-hand responses.

Kinaesthetic input from receptors in the muscles, joints, tendons and skin also provide essential information for development and refinement of fine-motor actions.

Why teach fine-motor?
Children explore the environment by moving and interacting with it. By manipulating objects and gathering valuable information about physical characteristics, they eventually gain the perceptual information necessary to make future judgements without the need for physical contact. Young children at school spend approximately 60–70% of their time completing fine-motor work or activities. Approximately 12% of children experience fine-motor skill difficulties.

Proficiency in fine-motor control allows the child to develop skills that will have consequences immediately and in later life and include:

SOCIAL CONSEQUENCES
Simple tasks such as tying laces or handling objects can cause frustration and embarrassment. The child who has poor fine-motor coordination begins to wonder why something that is natural and taken for granted is so difficult to perform.

VOCATIONAL CONSEQUENCES
Because a number of vocations, including secretarial work, dentistry, cabinet making, mechanical work and many others, have a large fine-motor component, the choices for the person with fine-motor difficulties begin to diminish.

ACADEMIC CONSEQUENCES
Quick and precise handling of concrete objects in mathematics, science and art become difficult. Precision and speed in hand-writing, keyboard striking and drawing tasks are minimised, affecting the amount of work being completed. Actions simply are not automatic; the available working memory and attentional space in the brain are taken up with concentrating on the movement rather than learning the concept.

PSYCHOLOGICAL (EMOTIONAL) CONSEQUENCES

Children with poor coordination often have unsuccessful experiences in physical activities. As a consequence, they can develop frustration, a fear of failure and rejection which, in turn, can lead to the development of a negative self-concept and avoidance behaviours, dramatically affecting classroom performance in all areas. Research tells us that a child's attitude towards learning, whether it be a fine-motor skill or learning to play basketball, is at least as important as a child's ability in that area!

This book provides several ideas for developing fine-motor skills in young children.

Motor memory

Motor memory has to do with your child's ability to visually and aurally copy single movements, movement patterns and rhythm patterns. Begin with just one movement, then increase according to one movement for each year of age. At first the child may just remember the moves in any order, but strive for correct sequencing of the moves. Playground equipment in your backyard or local park is ideal for 'memory touch' activities.

If the child experiences difficulties in this area, it may be appropriate to have a doctor check the child's eyesight and hearing.

Body management

Signals

Signals are quick one- to three-word phrases that draw the attention of the child almost immediately. For example, 'Iceberg!' or 'Freeze!' is the signal to stop immediately and listen; 'Hit the deck!' is the signal to quickly drop into front-lying position; 'Dead ant!' is the signal to get into back-lying position with arms and legs in the air. Through learning and reacting to these signals, the children develop better listening skills, alertness and reaction; improve in overall spatial and body awareness; develop good body management and control while moving or stationary; promote proper posture; develop and improve locomotion skills; enhance cooperation; and engage in activity to enhance their fitness.

Signals involve both a verbal and a visual signal and are categorised into *organisational* signals and *formation* signals. Once children have learned to react to these basic signals, then these become the 'management tools' for teaching fundamental movement skills, tasks and games. Furthermore, this concept can be extended to include the development of other signals, thus creating a movement language which can be constantly expanded. When the signals are well learned, the verbal signal can be taken away, so that only the visual signal is responded to. It may be necessary under certain conditions—for example, if you are teaching outside or using a lot of music inside the gymnasium—to use a whistle, which becomes the immediate attention grabber. Then the signal can be given, which becomes the indicator to do something. Once you become more confident and competent in using these tools, you will find yourself spontaneously creating more signals and usage. Enjoy the challenge!

Spatial awareness

Children have to learn to cope with near (personal) and far (general) space, otherwise many of the fundamental movement skills, such as throwing, catching and striking, will be more difficult to master.

PERSONAL SPACE, as the name suggests, is the immediate space within reach of a child's body parts. The child who continually bumps into things or knocks objects like the precious and valuable antique vase off the table, may be very likely displaying poor personal spatial skills.

GENERAL SPACE refers to the area in which a child or children and objects may move. Children who display poor evasive skills, who have difficulties in predicting the path of a ball or judging distances, are really displaying deficiencies in general space orientation. Within the understanding of space we have knowledge of directions, such as 'up' and 'down'; levels of space, such as 'high' and 'low'; distance relationships, such as 'near' and 'far'; and temporal aspects, such as judging the speed of objects moving through space. Also, children need to know and be able to demonstrate the different *stance positions* in personal space: *square*, *side-on* and *diagonal*.

Children need to understand spatial language both verbally and physically before they can successfully move around the environment. Following are the more common terms they need to know:

near/far   beside/away   under/over   up/down   in/out

square   side-on   diagonal

high/low   in front of/behind/next to   on/off

left/right   forwards/backwards/sideways   inside/outside

fast/slow   along/between   first/second/etc

face to face/back to back   front/middle/back   close to/far away

top/bottom   round/through   opposite side   open/close

shaking   shrugging   turning

tightening (tense)   stretching (extending)   bending (flexing)

swinging   sliding   rolling   lifting   touching

SHAPE LANGUAGE
circle   square   triangle   rectangle

SIZE LANGUAGE
big/bigger   small/smaller   little/large

TIME LANGUAGE
slow/slower   fast/faster   seconds

Body awareness

Children need to have an understanding of their own bodies. They need to know their body parts and where they are in relation to each other, including left- and right-sidedness (that is, left and right sides of the body) even though they might not be able to name them.

Emphasise good posture whenever possible, observe and offer comment.

Special considerations for children with special needs

Young children with an impairment or disability are generally as keen to participate in physical activity as the unimpaired. The Paralympics are testimony to the level of commitment and dedication that is achieved by many individuals perceived as being handicapped. It is often the restrictions that others place on these individuals that cause them to be viewed as handicapped or disabled. This section highlights special considerations for special populations. Below are definitions used to classify aspects of an individual's loss of physical/mental capacity.

IMPAIRMENT

This term is used to describe a loss or abnormality in physical, psychological or anatomical function.

DISABILITY

This term describes the lack of ability to perform an activity within considered normal ranges.

HANDICAP

This term refers to an impairment or disability which causes an individual to be disadvantaged in performing a normal role.

A child who has an impairment or disability does not necessarily need to be handicapped. There are many of these children who are only handicapped because of the physical or attitudinal barriers that society imposes. It is therefore essential, when planning for children with special needs, that we remind ourselves that without consideration and planning *we* may be the limiting factor, not the abilities of the child.

A multitude of terms have been used to describe the severity of disabilities; the danger with this is categorising children and subsequently having particular expectations rather than realistically evaluating what the individual is capable of achieving.

The key to working with children with a disability is to take each child on their merits. If this happens, the generalisations and goal setting that result in underachieving should not occur. Have a close look at rules, your method of instruction, the equipment you use and the environment you provide. Do not create a handicap.

ADAPTATIONS

Adaptations and modifications have to be made where appropriate, but only when necessary. The factors that need consideration when planning to work with an individual or a group of children with special needs include: method of instruction, time, environment/ space, equipment and rules.

Method of instruction may be
• mainly visual
• mainly auditory
• mainly kinaesthetic
• direct/in stages
• task orientated

Time may be
• increased to allow more time to achieve an outcome
• decreased to avoid unnecessary fatigue and possible injury
• alternated so that adequate periods of rest and activity can be established
• taken out as a factor altogether
• used as a goal and measurement of success or progress

Environment/space may be
• closed to make skills easier
• heated to reduce physical reaction to cold
• inside to reduce outside weather effects
• lightened to improve vision
• quietened to improve hearing/attention
• softened to reduce injury
• uncluttered so there is less chance of injury and distraction
• increased to allow freer movement
• decreased if fitness and/or movement is a concern
• marked by boundaries to assist spatial/organisational concepts
• specific (for example, a personal space) to provide security and/or assist spatial concepts

Equipment may be
• softer to avoid injury
• larger to make a task (such as catching, striking) easier
• colourful/different to promote attention
• lighter to allow easier movement
• shorter to decrease hand–eye error
• lower so it is easier to get over/in/on or off
• higher so it is easier to get under/through
• wider to make scoring easier

Rules may be modified to
• decrease competitive element
• allow more hits or misses
• allow players to sit instead of stand
• allow more bounces
• decrease distances to move
• eliminate restricting infringements

- increase player safety
- balance out ability differences
- allow runners
- increase substitutions
- increase/decrease number of players
- increase/decrease playing area

Below are some general considerations and implications for children with some of the more common disabilities. Please remember, however, that children with disabilities are like any other children. They are all different and bring with them individual abilities, so ensure you have knowledge of their condition, but treat them as individuals and maximise these abilities. *Individualise wherever possible.*

For most of the conditions described, you need to obtain information from organisations specifically concerned with the condition and from the child's medical practitioner as to the limitations and strengths that the child may have.

Intellectual/Learning disabilities

Attention deficit

SPECIAL CONSIDERATIONS

- Reduce outside distractions and keep the environment uncluttered and organised
- Break down instructions into single steps
- Use demonstration with instruction
- Create safe physical boundaries, for example, using cones and mats
- Establish routines
- Set short-term achievable goals
- Reward effort not just success

Down's syndrome

A child with Down's syndrome may display a number of physical features, but the only one they have in common is some degree of intellectual disability.

SPECIAL CONSIDERATIONS

- Consult with child's medical practitioner
- Reduce outside distractions and keep the environment uncluttered and organised
- Commence with a direct instruction that is clear and simple
- Use demonstration with instruction
- Create safe physical boundaries, for example, using cones and mats
- Establish routines
- Include strength and balance activities
- If atlantoaxial instability is present avoid stress on the head and neck regions
- If visual or auditory impairment is present appropriate strategies need to be employed

- Set short-term achievable goals
- Reward effort not just success

Autism

SPECIAL CONSIDERATIONS

- Reduce outside distractions and keep the environment uncluttered and organised
- Create safe physical boundaries, for example, using cones and mats
- Make sure there is a routine in activities. Concepts such as 'home' and other signals (described in Tune-up Session 5, (Organisation Signals, pages 64–66, Formation Signals, pages 66–68)) are extremely useful
- Only make very small changes to each new session
- Commence with a direct instruction that is clear and simple
- Use visual instruction such as demonstrations as often as possible
- Use physical rewards such as rubber stamps and clapping for effort and success

Physical disabilities

Obesity

This is becoming more common and is a functional disability. An obese child is affected both physically and psychologically and is often perceived as being lazy and their condition ignored. The consequences later for obesity may include cardiovascular disease, arthritis, diabetes and cancer.

SPECIAL CONSIDERATIONS

- Consider mobility, strength and flexibility limitations in the initial stages of the program
- Liaise with other significant people to include exercise as part of the total plan
- Because fitness is a concern, exercise bouts need to be initially shorter, slowly increasing in duration and intensity
- Set short-term achievable goals
- Reward effort, not just success

Asthma

This is the narrowing of the bronchial tubes causing difficulty in breathing. There are a number of factors that elicit this physiological reaction and the degree of asthma can vary from occasional to chronic.

SPECIAL CONSIDERATIONS

- Be familiar with the treatment of an asthma attack
- Consult with child's medical practitioner to assess physical limitations and what triggers an attack
- If necessary remind child to medicate before exercising

- Be aware of the triggers and the environment you are asking the child to exercise in
- Before commencing activities, ensure that the child has their medication on hand in case an attack occurs
- Avoid sudden temperature changes
- Be aware that long sustained activity may induce asthma in some children
- Swimming activities in a warm pool where the air is moist and humid are particularly good for children suffering asthma
- Activities that require the child to participate in short periods of exercise followed by a rest period should be preferred
- Exercises that promote correct breathing are excellent
- Allow adequate rest periods
- Set short-term achievable goals
- Reward effort, not just success

Spinal cord injury
Developed due to an accident, this includes paraplegia, quadriplegia and incomplete lesions.

SPECIAL CONSIDERATIONS
- Consult with child's medical practitioner to assess physical limitations
- Promote exercises that improve strength and flexibility
- Swimming pools are an excellent medium for completing strength and flexibility exercises
- Make sure access is available
- Because fitness is a concern, exercise bouts need to be initially shorter, slowly increasing the duration
- Set short-term achievable goals
- Reward effort, not just success

Cerebral palsy
A child with CP can display conditions that range from good functional strength with only minimal control difficulties to severe quadriplegia and spasticity.

SPECIAL CONSIDERATIONS
- Consult with child's medical practitioner to assess physical limitations
- Strength, balance and relaxation exercises are very important
- Adaptations to any physical activity need to be planned according to the functional limitations of the child
- CP children will have generally more success at exercises that involve large muscle groups
- Fine-motor programs should be a part of the program, but need to commence with larger movement activities such as finger painting, balloon play and rhythm sticks, progressing to finger isolation activities
- Set short-term achievable goals
- Reward effort, not just success

Muscular dystrophy
MD is an inherited disease characterised by progressive weakness of certain muscle groups.

SPECIAL CONSIDERATIONS
- Consult with child's medical practitioner to assess physical limitations
- Toning, flexibility and relaxation exercises are very important
- Strength exercises are useful for less severe conditions
- Breathing exercises are particularly useful
- Adaptations to any physical activity need to be planned according to the functional limitations of the child
- Swimming pools are an excellent medium for completing exercises
- Set short-term achievable goals
- Reward effort, not just success

Spina bifida
This is a developmental defect of the spine in which the vertebral arches have not fused, resulting in an abnormal gap.

SPECIAL CONSIDERATIONS
- Consult with child's medical practitioner to assess physical limitations and the position of the shunt (tube inserted to drain off excess cerebrospinal fluid)
- Be aware of the range of movement limitations in some throwing activities, contact, head activities, rolling and diving
- Progressive strength activities are important
- Some exercises will be best performed while sitting, some standing; be aware of the restriction of callipers
- Set short-term achievable goals
- Reward effort, not just success

Sensory impairment

Visual impairment
This includes the range from lack of peripheral vision to total blindness.

SPECIAL CONSIDERATIONS
- Ask what the child can see
- Environment has to be friendly and safe
- Describe the surroundings
- Large clear spaces in which to work
- Soft movable boundaries so that contact will not cause injury
- Well-lit and marked areas
- Ensure the child wears a safety strap to keep glasses secure on face or, even better, safety glasses
- Identify immovable objects that may cause injury

- Give appropriate feedback on the position of individual children in relation to objects
- Keep the layout consistent and try to make layouts familiar
- Limit visual demonstration; replace with verbal and kinaesthetic
- Assist physically whenever appropriate, for example, taking their arm to lead, directing their hand to an object
- Use objects that make a sound, such as bells in ball
- Set short-term achievable goals
- Reward effort, not just success

Hearing impairment
This includes children with slight to profound hearing loss.

SPECIAL CONSIDERATIONS
- Establish the degree of hearing loss
- Reduce background noise wherever possible
- Visual demonstration needs to be simple and progressive. The signals described on page 39 as well as Fit Session 5 (pages 64–68) are particularly useful
- Make sure you are facing the child when giving an instruction and speak normally
- Use activities that promote social skills
- Set short-term achievable goals
- Reward effort, not just success

IN SUMMARY
When working with children with special needs there are some key elements that need to be considered.
- Have a sound knowledge of the impairment/disability.
- Have a sound knowledge of the child's strengths and weaknesses.
- Safety is a key issue.
- Do not teach to the condition, teach the individual. These children are individuals who have to be taken on their merits. Individualise where possible.
- Only adapt if necessary and as little as required.
- If they are working with other children you have to ensure that inclusion occurs. This will require that the other children be taught understanding and acceptance.
- Plan ahead—know what you will teach.
- Be flexible and adaptable with rules, equipment, time and space.
- Allow the child to take responsibility and make choices.
- Set achievable goals.
- Reward effort and progress, not just success.
- Make sure you are not the handicap to a child progressing!

In summary

Now you are ready to get 'in motion'. Before you start with the activities just remember that children need to develop the skills and positive attitude to want to be active. As teachers or parents our responsibility lies in encouraging and helping to develop the habit of regular exercise. This goal is far more important than trying to train children to achieve a heart rate of 150 beats per minute over 30 minutes of exercise (this is an adult's perspective of exercise, not a child's!).

Kids with Zip contains a plethora of 'hands-on' practical and enjoyable ideas that can be implemented immediately in your existing or new program. Perhaps each of these ideas are 'seeds' that when germinated generate many more ideas of your own! Enjoy and grow with your child!

PART TWO

50 KIDS WITH ZIP SESSIONS

Basic skills—spatial awareness

1. Have children stand in tall position, feet shoulder-width apart, facing one wall of the room (or side of the play area). Demonstrate the square, side-on and diagonal stance positions. Have children copy you, then repeat using other walls (sides) as focal points. [Could trace child's feet on paper, cut out footprints and position in the different stance positions for child to stand on.]

2. Using objects in a room, have children move to music. When the music stops, ask children to move in relation to an object or piece of equipment or another person: e.g. stand in front of the chair; sit behind the ball; kneel beside the table.

3. In pairs, stand face-to-face; now back-to-back; side-by-side.

4. Use beanbag or small soft toy and have children place or throw object according to certain spatial commands: e.g. put beanbag on top of your head; place it behind you; put it beside you; in front of you; throw beanbag high.

5. Have children move in spaces to your directions without touching others or furniture/objects: e.g. move between objects; move around; move under; move on and off; move through. Move along a rope; travel between the ladder rungs. Run around the tree; move through the big tyre.

6. Have children move in spaces using different ways of travelling (locomotion): e.g. walking, sliding, hopping, skipping. Now have them move in different directions, such as walking backwards; sliding sideways; skipping forwards.

7. Have children move to music in different directions, at different speeds: e.g. walking quickly backwards; skipping slowly forwards.

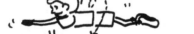

8. Have children move in spaces at different levels. Then think up combinations of locomotion, level, direction and speed: e.g. creeping medium level, backwards slowly; rolling, low level, sideways quickly.

9. Begin to add left and right concepts to the above activities: e.g. 3 hops forwards with left foot; 3 hops forwards with right foot; three steps to left; pass by an object on the right side; touch another object with your left foot; place beanbag on the right side of you; toss beanbag with your right hand and catch it with left; bounce a ball on the right side with the right hand; bounce in front with left hand.

10. Have one partner do one thing while the other partner does the opposite: e.g. one in front of something, the other behind; one on something, other off; move over something, while partner moves under; stand up, partner sit down.

11. Be high, be low; roll along the ground.

12. Move in a big circle, make your circle become smaller and smaller; larger and larger. Travel a square pathway; rectangular pathway; triangular pathway.

13. *Two-way/Four-way traffic*
    Have 4 teams of 4–6 children position on a different side of the play area (square). Assign the teams numbers, 1, 2, 3 and 4. See diagram. Signal teams to move across the square in different ways and from a variety of starting positions:
    • 1 and 3—power walk; 2 and 4—power walk
    • 4 and 2—jog; 3 and 1—jog
    • 1 and 3—puppy dog walk; 2 and 4—puppy dog walk
    • 4 and 2—crab walk; 3 and 1—crab walk
    • 1 . . . 2 . . . 3 . . . 4—skipping!
    Front-lying position with head on the line:
    • 1 and 3—kangaroo jumps; 2 and 4—kangaroo jumps
    • 4 and 2—bunny hops; 3 and 1—frog leaps

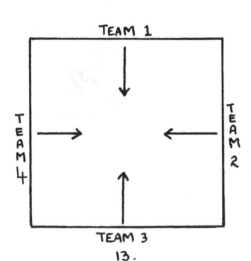

14. *Vertical ladders (climbing frame)*

    Have children move between the rungs of a ladder according to your instruction: move one foot, then one hand; move up, move down, move across, move through; then use right/left concepts, such as move right hand then left foot as you climb upwards; and so on.

14.

15. *Grid patterns*

    Using carpet squares or marking out a grid pattern with masking tape, give signals for child to move: start in square 1; make 2 hops up; 3 jumps to the right; take one step backwards; touch your right hand to the square beside you; put your left foot in the square in front of you; make 3 jumps diagonally downwards. Give children a 'directions' map to follow different patterns on this grid.

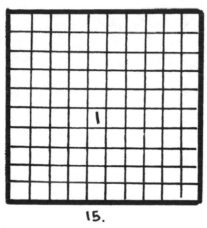

15.

16. *Shadow dodging*

    Children in pairs take turns being the leader and the 'shadow' as they move around the play area. Encourage leader to make quick changes of direction (dodging) and the 'shadow' to stick as close to the leader as possible! On signal (one whistle blow) children immediately jump-stop. Praise good 'stops!' The leader and shadow change roles and continue the activity. Call out different locomotion movements each time they move again: walking, running, skipping, hopping, slide-stepping.

16.

17. *Obstacle courses*

    Children move over/under; on/off; through, across, around, between, and so on. Create an obstacle course with your child; draw a map which shows how you will move through the obstacle course.

OVER   UNDER

17.

18. *The choo-choo train*

You are the engine; the end child is the caboose, and the children in between are the cars. The train moves along the railway tracks (lines on the gym floor or boundary lines), weaving in and out of traffic cones. Use arm actions to simulate the wheels turning; make sounds of the train chugging along and whistle blowing.

19. *'Ship ahoy!'*

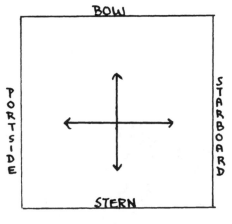

Let's turn the play area into a giant ship. Face square on to this wall (or boundary line). This is the *bow* of the ship. Your back is now facing the *stern* of the ship. As you face the bow, the right side of the ship is called *starboard*; left side, *portside*.

• Jump-turn to face each side of the ship as I call the name out: starboard, stern, portside, bow.

• Start in your 'home' space and move to the front, back or side, listening to what is called out.

• Now add other signals to this game. For example: 'Jump to the bow! Iceberg! Dead bug!' 'Jog to the stern—periscope!' (back-lying position with one knee straight up into the air and hold). 'Walk backwards to starboard! Rescue!' (quickly find a partner and grab each other's wrist of one hand and gently pull). 'Slide-step to portside. Hit the deck! Now please "scrub" the deck.' 'Skip to bow, in twos back-to-back. Do the "siamese crab walk"' lean forwards and grab each other's wrists between your legs. Now walk in this way).

SIAMESE CRAB WALK

20. *In the jungle*

Start in your home space. Check for good spacing. Take children on a safari using different movements such as:

• stepping over tall grass (low hurdles)
• moving under the bridge (hurdles, table, chair)
• wading across the stream (giant steps)
• jumping off a rock (box horse)
• sneaking up behind a tree to watch the zebras eating grass
• crawling through a cave (hoops or 4 chairs in a file)

- walking across a suspended bridge (balance beam or bench)
- climbing up a tree, grabbing a vine, swinging out to splash in river
- sitting cross-legged in front of the fire playing African drums
- miming a native jungle animal or bird or reptile.

21. *Shuttle relays*

    Shuttle formation—split each group of 4–6 players so that 2–3 stand in one file facing the opposite file of 2–3, spaced 10 giant steps apart.

    - Run to opposite side giving high 10s for the next player to go.
    - Run to the opposite side bouncing a ball to the next player in line.
    - Run to the opposite side dribbling a ball to the next player in line.
    - Zig-zag through the markers to the opposite line.
    - Do different locomotion movements: slide-step, walk backwards, skip, hop.
    - Do different animal walks.
    - Use a jump-hoop to travel to the other side.

    20.

21.

Basic skills—body awareness

1. Have children point to the body part you name, first with eyes open, then with eyes closed. Repeat, having children point and name the body part.

ELBOW 1. KNEE

2. Have one child lie down in back-lying position on a large piece of paper or pavement. Use a marking pen (or chalk) to trace the outline of the child's body. Have children in turn point and name the body parts. Have children in turn write the names of the body parts.

2.

BLINK...
3.

HEAR...

3. Ask questions such as: 'What body part do you . . . smell with? Talk with? Hear with? Blink with? Clap with? Point with? Wave with? Jump with?'

4. Have children move to music. When the music stops, jump-stop and touch the body part called out. (Vary the way the children move.)

5. Ask children to: 'clap your hands'; 'snap your fingers'; 'blink one eye, then the other, then both'; 'gently turn your head from side to side'; 'stamp your feet'; 'point your foot upwards'; 'wiggle your bottom'; 'shake-shake-shake' all over.

5.

6.

RIGHT KNEE TO
LEFT ELBOW

6. Now try directional actions such as: open and close your right hand; lift your left knee; raise your right elbow; circle your right arm; balance on your left foot; touch right knee to left elbow; hold your left foot with your right hand.

7. Have children in standing position, cross arms and legs, right over left and sit down; then stand up again without undoing this body position. Repeat crossing left over right arms and legs.

7.

ELBOW TO ELBOW

8.

LEFT FOOT TO LEFT FOOT

8. *Busy body parts*
Children walk around in general space in and out of each other. 'Scrambled eggs, walking . . . Freeze!' Everyone jump-stops and listens for the body part signal. Call out the name of a body part, 'Elbows!' Children quickly partner up and touch elbow to elbow. Call out the name of another body part, 'Knees!' Children must now find a new partner and touch knees. Continue in this way.

VARIATIONS
• Call out the name of two body parts such as 'knee and elbow'.
• Touch right parts to right parts; left parts to left parts; right parts to left parts.
• Touch 3 different body parts.

9. *Busy muscles*

Call out name of a muscle, for example, 'hamstrings' (back thigh muscles). Children find a partner and touch hamstrings. Call out another muscle, for example, 'biceps' (top muscles of upper arm). Now each one must find a new partner and touch this muscle.

Other muscles: quadriceps (front muscles of thigh); deltoids (shoulder muscles); triceps (underneath muscles of lower arm); gluteus maximus (buttock muscles).

HAMSTRING TO HAMSTRING

9.

TRICEPS TO TRICEPS

10. *Busy bones*

Call out the name of a bone, for example, 'patella' (knee cap). Partners then touch knee caps. Call out the name of another bone, 'femur' (upper leg—longest bone). Now children find a new partner and touch femurs. Continue in this way.

Other bones: cranium (bones of head), clavicle (collar bone), scapula (shoulder blade), humerus (upper arm bone), ribs, phalanges (finger and toe bones).

VARIATION:

Touch the muscle or bone with an object such as a beanbag.

10.

PHALANGES

PATELLA TO PATELLA

11. *Busy letters and numbers*

INDIVIDUAL
- Make the letter 'L', 'Y', 'O', 'T', 'C'
- Make the following numbers: 1, 6, 7, 0

PARTNERS
- Make the letter 'A', 'P', 'D', 'H', 'X'
- Make the following numbers: 3, 6, 8, 17
- Make two-lettered words

THREES
- Triangles, circles, squares, diamonds
- Make different letters
- Make different numbers—single, double and triple digits
- Make

"X"

"TRIANGLE"

11.

"L"

"Y"   "T"

"6"   "17"

"F   I   T"

Basic skills—motor memory activities

1. *Copy me*
   - Have children copy hand movements: palms up, palms down; hands up, hands down; hands sideways.
   - Have children copy body movements: arm circling, hands on head, knee lifts, seat circles, leg shakes, different facial expressions.
   - Have children copy clapping rhythms: finger-snapping, foot stamping, hand-clapping, hand and foot clap and stamp.
   - Play 'Follow-the-leader' around the playground.

2. *Simon says*
   When you say 'Simon says ...' children respond by doing the task; when you ask children to do a task without first saying 'Simon says ...', children do not respond. How good a listener can you be? For example, 'Simon says ... wiggle your left fingers'; 'stamp your feet!' 'Simon says ... click your right fingers'; 'blink with your left eye'.

3. *Touch*
   - Copying touching movements to different body parts: touch your right elbow to your left knee; right hand on hip and left hand holding left ankle behind.
   - Have children touch different body parts in order: hand—knee—toe; touch 3 different objects in order: chair—table—door; touch elbow to fence—nose to tree—shoulder to swing.

4. *Memory order game*
   Have children form groups of 5–6. In each group, children take turns being 'it' in playing the game. The group selects 5 objects and the order that the objects are to be touched by 'it'. The objects and order could be different for each game played. Use playground objects or scatter several objects in the play area.

5. *Animal charades*

Ask children to pick their favourite animal. Point to different children asking them in turn to act out their animal. The other children try to guess the name of it, then everyone mimics the mimer.

5.

6. *Alphabet arms*

On a large piece of paper write the letters of the alphabet using upper case letters. Underneath each letter write an 'L or 'R' or 'B'. Choose one colour for the letters of the alphabet and another colour for the movement letters. For 'L' have children extend left arms to the side; for 'R', extend right arms to side; for 'B', extend both arms out in front. Have children say the letter and do the associated arm movement with that letter. Encourage children to progress at their own rate. Observe actions and the saying of the letters. Practise part by part, slowly, until children have mastered each part. Challenge children by asking them to do this activity backwards or from right to left.

VARIATIONS

- Use upper case, lower case, different fonts.
- Change the actions used: for example, underneath each letter write 'C' or 'F' or 'S'. For 'C' have children clap hands together; for 'F', click fingers in the air; for 'S', slap knees with hands.
- Randomly mix the letters and arm movements.
- For younger children use pictures, shapes or colours instead of letters.

7. *The eye box*

On a large poster or flip chart draw a large rectangular box as shown. Tell the children that this is an 'eye box.' In the box use a different coloured marking pen to indicate the following locations: top right, top middle, top left, bottom right, bottom middle, bottom left. Ask children to stand tall in a home space. Make sure that they can all see the eye box. Call out different locations and have children move only their eyes to those places. Emphasise that they keep their head still and move only their eyes. Observe their actions and comment.

Note:

Locations are put on the box right to left as the child looks square-on to the box.

VARIATIONS:

- For younger children use pictures of well-known animals.
- Use basic colours: red, orange, yellow, green, blue and purple for the locations.
- Have each child draw their own eye box and then use it for letting their eyes move to the locations called.
- Now have them imagine an eye box in front of them. Call out different locations.

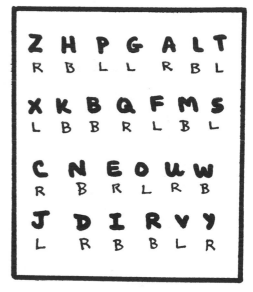

VARIATION: RANDOM MIX OF ALPHABET LETTERS

6.

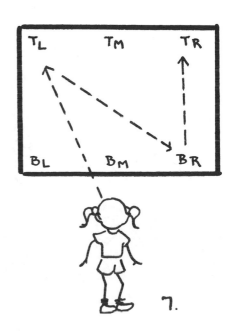

7.

8. *Music ball mirror*

Use music to help develop a sense of rhythm. Children each hold a medium- to small-sized ball in both hands. Stand facing the children making sure that everyone can see you. Begin moving the ball slowly around different parts of the body. Children copy your movements.

- Toss the ball back and forth from hand to hand.
- Circle around your waist; around your knees.
- Do large body circles.
- Move the ball in a figure-8 in and out of your legs.
- Stretch with the ball overhead; to the side; down low.

Basic skills—balancing

Children may need some support when doing these balancing activities. Try to get them to 'feel' their body position by closing their eyes. Each balance should be held for 10 seconds and repeated at least 3 times until you observe that the child has control.

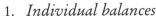

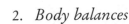

1. *Individual balances*
   - Balance on one foot, with your hands out to the sides.
     Hold for 10 second count. Balance on the other foot.
     Hold for 10 second count.
     Repeat, but with eyes closed.
   - How many different ways can you balance on:
     front, back, side, sitting, knees. Try with eyes closed.
   - Balance on different body combinations (points):
     two hands and one knee (3 points);
     two knees, two elbows (4 points);
     one hand and opposite foot (2 points).
   - Make a bridge using different body parts.
   - Make up a balance of your own!
   - Balance on your hands and kick your feet up in the air.
     (May need to spot children as they become inverted!)

2. *Body balances*
   Find your home space.
   - Show me how you make a 2 point shape other than just using your feet (3 point shape; 4 point shape; 5 point shape).
   - Make a long shape; a wide shape; a twisted shape; a curled shape.
   - Find a partner: repeat the tasks above.
   - Groups of 3—make 3 point, 4 point, 5 point, 6 point and 7 point shapes.

3. *Balancing games*

3.

- **STATUES**

  Have children move in different ways to music. When the music stops, call out a number '1, 2, 3 . . .' Children jump-stop and immediately perform a balance on the number of points called out.

- **BALANCING CIRCLES**

  Children move around in a large play area to music. Draw or mark out circles, or scatter hoops throughout the play area. When the music stops, call out a number that indicates to the children that they must form a group of that size in the circle—all supporting each other as they stand on one leg!

4. *Equipment balancing*

  - Balance with feet on 2 dome markers or wooden blocks as shown.
  - Now balance with one leg on one dome marker or wooden block.
  - Balance on the other leg.
  - Repeat with eyes closed.
  - Balance walk on a line or along a rope stretched on the floor.
  - Walk along bench or a beam from one end to the other. Jump off. Remember to bend at the knees. Keep your arms out sideways to help you balance.
  - Explore other ways of moving along the bench: kneel, stand up, turn around; small jumps; catch a ball and walk along the beam; walk on all fours; slide on your back; slide on your front; walk with one foot on the bench, other off.

4.

SLIDE ON FRONT   WALK - JUMP OFF!

EQUIPMENT AVAILABLE AT TOY STORES

- Explore balancing on a homemade balance board or duck walker. Try to rock side to side; walk like a duck.
- Explore balance walking on stilts or bucket steppers as shown.
- Balance and hop on a Lolo™ ball.
- Balance and hop on a Pogobouncer™.

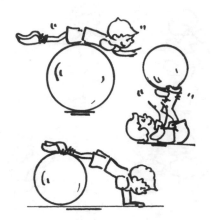

5. *Slo-Mo™ play*

Use the Slo-Mo™ Ball or Gymnic™ Ball in station play. Explore balancing/weight supporting using the ball.

• Balance on your tummy.
• Balance on your back.
• Balance the ball by holding it high with your feet while lying on your back.
• Balance with feet on the ball and hands on floor, head down.
• Balance with feet on the ball and hands on floor, head up.
• Balance while trying to sit on the ball.
• Bounce the ball in place.
• Bounce the ball through an obstacle course.
• Balance the ball between 2 players and try to move in different directions.
• Partners in long-sit position, back-to-back with the Slo-Mo™ Ball between them, then try to stand up without letting the ball drop away.
• Use the smaller balls to roll into targets or bowl over targets.

Basic skills—body management—Signals

The following Signals provide ways of effectively mobilising children and developing their listening skills and spatial awareness. Identify the boundaries of the play area that children will move around in. Use at least 8 cone markers spaced evenly apart around the area. Establish the following Signals that children can quickly learn and respond to. Single-out good listeners and praise them!

Organisation Signals

1. *'Home!'* (Hand Signal—make a roof overhead with hands.)

Mats, hoops, carpet squares or deck rings could also be used as 'homes'. Find a free space in the play area. Check that you cannot touch anyone or anything. This is your 'home!'—remember it. Now leave your home and touch 5 different markers, with 5 different body parts. Return to 'stand tall' in your home space. Go!

2. *'Scrambled eggs!'* (Hand Signal—roll hand over hand.)

   Listen carefully to how I will ask you to move. Then move in this way: in and out of each other, without touching anyone, for example, *'Scrambled eggs—walking!'*

3. *'Freeze!' or 'Iceberg!'* (Hand Signal—raise one hand in the air with thumb up.)

   This is your stopping Signal. When you hear or see this word, stop immediately by 'jump-stopping' (landing on both feet at the same time, knees bent, hands out for balance).

4. *'Quiet!'* (Hand Signal—raise one hand overhead.)

   This is your 'stop–look–listen' Signal. Stop what you are doing and raise your hand overhead, giving me your full attention!

5. *'Dead bug!'* (Hand Signal—thumbs down.)

   Quickly and safely lie on your back, raise your arms and legs in the air and wiggle them gently.

6. *'Hit the deck!'* (Hand Signal—point index fingers of both hands to the ground.)

   This is your Signal to drop carefully to the ground, in front-lying position. Stay there until you hear the next Signal.

7. *'Clear the deck!'* (Hand Signal—raise both hands in the air and out to the sides.)

   Move quickly to stand outside on one side of the marked play area. Clear the deck again! Now move to stand outside another side. Continue in this way. (Vary the way children move: slide-step, skip, run high, walk low.)

8. *'Islands!'* (Hand Signal—teacher uses both hands to draw a square shape in the air.)

   This is a group/team learning square which can vary in formation, size and number. Cone markers, ropes, 1.3 m × 2 m (4 ft × 6 ft) light carry mats, signs and so on can be used to indicate each island location and space. Each islander can still find a 'home' (individual learning space) within their island.

Teacher can designate one square to be the 'Main island' (the teaching square—see the example below). Each team or group moves to its designated island taking the necessary equipment along and sets up as instructed.

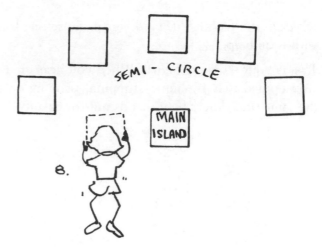

Formation Signals

Formation Signals effectively and efficiently organise the children into location and position. If teaching the children outside, ensure that they are not looking directly into the sun and use markers to clearly indicate the boundaries of the play area.

1. *'Listening line'* (Hand Signal—arms outstretched sideways as you stand near and facing line.)

    Use the boundaries of the play area. Immediately run and stand in a long line where I am pointing. Face me and space yourself an arm's length apart. Now take giant steps across to the opposite side and stand on a listening line once there. How many giant steps did you take? Return to your listening line, again counting the number of steps.

2. *'Listening circle'* (Hand Signal—point with index finger to the floor near you while circling the other index finger overhead.)

    Run quickly and safely to cross-leg sit in the circle that I am pointing to and face me.

3. *'Listening corner'* (Hand Signal—cross your arms making the letter 'X', then point to the corner with your index finger.)

   Run quickly and safely to cross-leg sit in this corner and face me.

4. *'End line'* (Hand Signal—arms outstretched to sides, with fingers of hand facing upwards.)

   Run quickly and safely to stand on end line that I am pointing to and face me. Check for good spacing.

END LINE   4.

5. *'Groups of 2!, 3!'* (Hand Signal—indicate group size by showing that number of fingers, followed by the 'Home!' Hand Signal.)

   Children quickly sit in a group indicated by the number of fingers shown.

6. *'Teams!'* (Hand Signal—both hands held out in front parallel to ground as you stand near a designated line.)

   Children quickly fall into their teams, with the captain at the front and the co-captain at the end of each team.

   Everyone cross-leg sits in file formation (one behind the other).

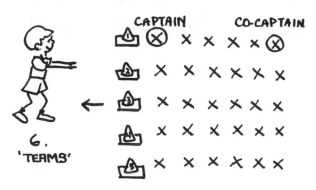

6.
'TEAMS'

CAPTAIN   CO-CAPTAIN

7. *'Waves!'* (Teacher moves from facing the file to position on either side as shown in diagram.)

   Children, in stand tall position, space themselves an arm's length apart, with each wave on a designated floor line or 3 giant steps away from the wave in front.

7.
'WAVES'

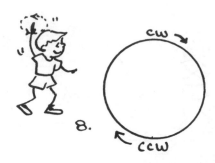

8. *'Circle up!'* (Hand Signal—hand raised overhead, circling in a CW (clockwise) or CCW (counter/anti-clockwise) direction.)

Children run in a CW (or CCW) direction, single file, around the play area.

9. *'Snake!'* (Hand Signal—Listening line Hand Signal, then point to line of direction, such as a wall.)

Children quickly run to stand on the listening line, then turn to file formation (one behind the other), facing the direction the teacher indicates. Children stay in this file order as they move.

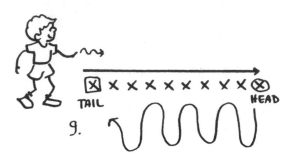

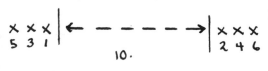

10. *'Shuttle!'* (Hand Signal—use the Team Hand Signal and then split the team into 2 groups.)

Each team splits into 2 groups who stand in file formation, each half facing the other and spaced a designated distance apart.

Basic skills—body management— starting and stopping, falling and posture

Starting and stopping activities

Children need to learn how to control their bodies at an early age so that they will not get physically hurt and their confidence will continue to improve, as well as their alertness, reaction and ability to respond quickly. These skills may even save your child's life in a threatening situation. Observe children when they stop—are they in control? Do they fall over? Do they stop immediately? Offer good praise and encouragement.

• Have children run for 5 seconds, then 'jump-stop' (both feet touch the ground at the same time, feet are shoulder-width apart, knees bent). This is the safest way to stop.

- Have children run in general space, changing direction often. On your signal 'Freeze!' children stop immediately. Observe their stopping action. Insist that they jump-stop!
- Repeat, having children move in different ways: walking, hopping, skipping, jogging, sliding, moving backwards, moving on all fours.
- Use music to start and stop children.
- Now have them partner up. One partner follows the other like a shadow. On signal 'Freeze!' both come to a jump-stop. If the partner behind can touch the partner in front, change roles. Continue in this way.

Falling activities

These activities teach children how to land safely when falling and prevent injury. Ideally, do on a soft surface such as a mat or carpet, otherwise grass will do.

- From kneeling position, fall forwards. Take weight on hands, bending arms to stop you before your stomach touches the mat. Keep your hands flat, fingers slightly inwards and back straight.
- Repeat from kneeling position, fall forwards and roll.
- From squat position, fall forwards.
- Repeat from squat position, but this time fall forwards and roll.
- From standing tall position, fall forwards like a tree. 'Timber . . .!'
- Repeat 'Timber!' and add roll as soon as contact with hands is made.
- Dominoes. Have several children or family members kneel beside each other, spaced about a giant step apart. On signal 'Dominoes!', first player falls forwards, immediately followed by the second, then the third, and so on. Repeat from a standing position.

Sideways falling activities

- From a kneeling position, fall sideways to rock onto your arm first, then side and shoulder. Fall sideways in one direction; then in the other.
- Fall down a grassed slope rolling sideways.
- From a standing position, do a forwards shoulder roll: roll onto your lower arm, then upper arm, shoulder, back and up onto your feet.

More falling activities

These activities teach your child how to fall backwards safely to prevent injury. Ideally, do on a soft surface such as a mat or carpet, otherwise grass will do.

> **FIT TIP**
>
> Children need to learn to make good landings at an early age to absorb force of landing, avoid jarring of body joints and prevent injury.

• From a sitting position rock backwards. Let your arms take your weight.
• From a standing position, squat down and fall backwards, rocking onto your back.
• Stand, fall backwards, rock onto your back, rock forwards and stand again.
• Jump up, land bending your knees, rock backwards, rock forwards to stand and spring upwards again. Repeat.

Posture positions

The following positions emphasise good posture and, at the same time, provide an efficient way of getting children in the appropriate body position for the demands of the skill, activity or game. Observe children carefully, correct posture as needs be, and encourage and praise their efforts!

1. *Stand tall*
   Stand with feet comfortably spread apart and toes turned out slightly. Arms are at the sides, hands relaxed, eyes looking forwards.

2. *Cross-leg sit*
   Sit with legs crossed and arms resting on the knees.

3. *Long-sit*
   Sit with legs outstretched and together. Lean back on your hands for support.

4. *Hook-sit*
   Sit with legs together, bent at knees and feet flat on the floor. Lean back to take weight on hands.

5. *Half-hook-sit*
   Sit with one leg outstretched and the other leg bent. Lean back to support weight on hands.

6. *Wide-sit*
   Sit with legs outstretched and comfortably apart. Lean back on hands for support.

7. *All fours*

Support your weight on hands and knees, facing downwards.

7.

8. *Knee sit*

Sit upright on your knees, hands resting on your knees.

KNEELING SIT
Sit back on your knees.

8.

9. *One knee up, one knee down*

Sit with one knee up and the other knee down as shown. Keep your back straight.

9.

10. *Front-lying position*

Lie face down with your legs extended backwards and together, arms by your sides at chest level.

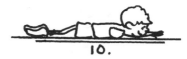
10.

11. *Front support position*

Support weight on hands and toes, facing downwards. Hold body straight.

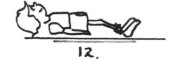
11.

12. *Back-lying position*

Lie facing upwards, legs straight and arms at sides.

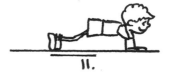
12.

13. *Back support position*

From hook-sit position, take weight on hands and feet raising body off the floor; keep legs straight and extended, arms slightly bent at elbow.

13.

14. *Hook-lying position*

Lie on back with knees bent so that weight is on feet and arms are relaxed at the sides.

14.

15. *Squat position*

From standing position, bend knees to raise heels off the floor. Place hands between your legs and rest them on the floor.

15.

Posture activities

1. Stand tall. Sit tall. Back straight, head up, eyes looking forwards. Walk 'tall'.

1.

2. Have children walk around the play area balancing a beanbag or throwing ring on their heads.

3. In a home space, with the bean bag on their head, ask them to move from stand tall position to hook-sit position, to stand tall again.

4. Again move them around the play area by jogging (skipping, sliding, walking, and so on). Call out 'Freeze!', wait and observe that they jump-stop; then ask them to get into one of the posture positions. Continue in this way.

5. Let yourself hang on the horizontal bar and stretch your whole body!

6. *Puppets*
You are a puppet and I will pull certain strings to make you move, such as: raising and lowering your right arm; lifting your left knee; making your head bend forwards and gently back; stamping your feet; shaking yourself gently all over; then making yourself floppy so that you 'plop' gently to the ground.

Fit Session 1

Walking activities

As children's fitness increases, gradually speed up the pace of the activities. Remember to use 'Freeze!' as the stop signal.
• Forwards, backwards, sideways
• On toes, on heels
• Quickly, slowly, quick changes of direction, change of pace
• Big steps, baby steps, feet close together, feet wide apart
• Straight, curved, zig-zag, figure-8, circle, rectangle
• Walk as if you are happy, angry, excited, frightened, sad
• Walk to music with a steady 4/4 beat
• Do marching steps and clap hands in time to music

Games

1. *'Follow-the-leader'*
Use the above activities.

2. *'Here, where, there'*

On 'Here!', walk towards me; on 'Where!', walk on the spot; on 'There!', walk away from me. (Use other locomotion movements such as jogging, skipping, side-stepping.)

'HERE!'

2.

3. *'Memory walk'*

Give children 3 or 4 walking tasks to do in the order given or in any order. Ask children to listen carefully before moving. For example: walk to touch 3 lines; then touch 2 opposite walls; and finish with touching 2 circles. Walk to touch 3 trees; then walk to touch 3 different pieces of playground equipment.

3.

FIT FOCUS: STRENGTH

Visit a local park that has a playground station with lots of interesting apparatus. Encourage children to explore all parts of it: hanging, climbing, swinging, balancing, sliding. When the child is performing inverted hanging activities (hanging by the legs) let the child take their body weight; but always take the precaution of holding onto the child. Suggest always spotting the child for any hanging activities.

Set challenges to perform:
• Can you hang for 10 seconds while I count 1, 2, 3, . . .?
• Show me how you can climb to the top. Careful!
• Can you swing across on the flying fox?
• How many different ways can you move down the slide?

FIT FOCUS: FLEXIBILITY

'Dead bug stretches'

Pretend that you are a 'dead bug' and lie on your back with your feet and hands in the air. Holding your ankles and keeping your legs straight, gently stretch towards your head. Stretch by holding opposite hand to opposite ankle. Repeat using other hand. (Can use right and left terms.)

" DEAD BUG!"

'Angels in the snow'

In back-lying position, spread your legs and arms apart, then together. Now just spread your legs apart; then just arms. Repeat with just one side moving away; then other side.

Fit Session 2

8

BOUNDARY LINE

FIGURE-8

SPRINT   WALK

FIT FOCUS: AEROBIC

Remember to use the stopping signal 'Freeze!'

Running activities

- Jog on the spot; jog straight ahead
- Jog along the outside boundary of the basketball court
- Jog slowly; jog quickly; jog changing speed on my signal
- Run with quick changes of direction (dodging) on my signal
- Jog up the hill; jog down the hill
- Jog around a large rectangle path, power walking the short sides and running as fast as you can along the long sides
- Jog in a big figure-8
- Jog in time to the music, changing direction every 8 beats; clap your hands when you change direction
- Jog lightly; jog heavily
- Run as fast as you can for 10 seconds; then walk for 10 seconds. Repeat this pattern
- Jog to touch the objects that I name: tree, fence, goal post, line

FIT FOCUS: AEROBIC/AGILITY

1. *Follow me jog*
   Children follow you around the playground, around trees, over and under obstacles, on and off obstacles.

2. *Changing speed*
   Space 4 markers at 10 metres/yards apart. Have child run quickly to the first marker; slowly to the next; quickly to the next; and slowly to the finish. Repeat.

← RUN → ← RUN → ← RUN →
QUICKLY   SLOWLY   QUICKLY

FIT FOCUS: STRENGTH/BALANCE

1. *Combative play*
   - **HAND PUSH**
     Partners stand facing, with one foot slightly forwards and knees bent. Partners then push against the palms of each other's hands.
   - **TUG OF WAR**
     Partners, using a finger grip, pull against each other. Use right hands; then left hands.
   - **TOWEL TUG OF WAR**
     Use a towel gripped in both hands, pull against each other.

TOWEL TUG OF WAR

2. *Hoppo bumpo*

   Stand on one leg facing each other with arms crossed. Each partner tries to 'bump' the other partner off balance.

HOPPO BUMPO

FIT FOCUS: FLEXIBILITY

1. *Head and eye stretch*

   Let your eyes look in one direction as your head turns gently from one side to the other. Keep your head still as your eyes look upwards, then downwards, to one side, to the other side. Let your eyes trace a large circle in front of you; a figure-8.

2. *Belly-button swivels*

   Standing tall, with your feet shoulder-width apart, trace a large circle with your belly-button. Circle 4 times one way, then circle 4 times the other way. Poke your belly-button in, then poke it out.

Fit Session 3

FIT FOCUS: AEROBIC

1. *Rectangle running*

   Mark out a rectangle that is 6 m × 10 m. Have children run the lengths of the rectangle and power walk the widths. Repeat running in the opposite direction.

2. *Figure-8*

   Place 2 cone markers about 15 metres/yards apart. Have children run in a figure-8 pattern around the cones. How many times can each one complete the pattern in 30 seconds?

3. *Zig-zag running*
   Set out about 6 markers 2–3 metres/yards apart. Have children zig-zag between the markers and return. Ask them to travel in different ways: forwards, sideways by slide-stepping, backwards, power-walking

4. *Activity lines*
   Mark off 4 lines that are spaced 10 metres/yards apart. Have children: jog forwards to the first line, jog backwards to the starting line; jog forwards to the second line, jog backwards to the starting line; jog forwards to the third line, and then again backwards to the start. How fast can they do this?

FIT FOCUS: STRENGTH

Fling-it play
(Use a beach towel, a 2 m (6 ft) parachute, a sheet or a Fling-It® Net.)
- Place a small object, such as a soft ball, beanbag or a small soft toy in the centre and shake the object up and down.
- 'POPCORN'—Shake several light objects off the towel.
- Plant your feet and, at the same time, pull away from the towel. Repeat with your back to the towel.
- Slide-step in a circle holding onto the towel and leaning away.
- Make up another activity to do with your towel; for example, roll up towel, plant your feet and have a 'tug of war'.

FIT FOCUS: FLEXIBILITY

Stretching shapes

Name a shape then have children hold that shape for 5–10 seconds. Examples:

• a wide shape like the letter 'Y' or 'T'
• round shape–like a ball
• long shape–like a pencil
• curved shape–like the letter 'C' or a banana
• twisted shape–like a pretzel

BALL

PENCIL

CURVED

TWISTED

FIT TIP

Your 'biceps' are the muscles of your upper arm. They are needed to help you lift and carry things, to throw objects, to swim, to use the parachute!

Fit Session 4

FIT FOCUS: AEROBIC

Can you?

• Move like a prancing horse
• Move like a speedboat or jet ski, cutting through the waves
• Move like an ice-skater or a figure skater
• Move like a hawk swooping down on a small animal
• Move like a snow-boarder or skier over moguls
• Move like a Boeing 747 taking off down the runway
• Move like a kite dipping and lifting in the air
• Move like a lawn-mower cutting the grass
• Move like a busy bee flitting from flower to flower

PRANCING HORSE

FIGURE SKATER

SNOW-BOARDER

BOEING 747

BOXER

KARATE
KID

FIT FOCUS: STRENGTH

1. *Shadow boxer*
   Pretend you are a boxer. Show me how you can punch into the air. Make your feet 'dance'.
2. *Karate kid*
   Use your arms to slash through the air and your feet to kick.

3. *Bucking bronco*
   Take your weight on your hands and kick your feet into the air.

BUCKING BRONCO

FIT FOCUS: FLEXIBILITY

1. *Sunflower*
   Begin curled up into a tight ball. Slowly start to uncurl and open up to a standing position with your arms in the air. Take a 10-second count to end on tiptoes. Now take 10 seconds to return to a tight curled position as low to the ground as you can go. Repeat.

'Sunflower'

2. *Imagery—R-E-L-A-X*
   Lie on a mat in back-lying position and relax. Think of something that is very pleasant, that will bring a smile to your face. Listen to the quiet background music. Breathe slowly. Relax—let yourself just go.
   • Now tense just your hands for a 3-second count, then relax. Tense again, relax.
   • Tense your face—relax.
   • Tense your shoulders—relax.
   • Tense your stomach muscles—relax.
   • Tense your seat muscles—relax.
   • Tense your legs and feet—relax.
   • Tense all over! Let everything go limp—relax.
   • Tense all over again—relax.

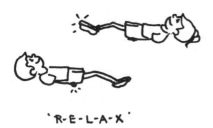

'R-E-L-A-X'

Fit Session 5—shallow water activities

FIT FOCUS: AEROBIC

In shallow water (about knee/waist depth):
- Face child on opposite sides of the pool. Walk across the pool to change places.
- Repeat, but this time zig-zag your way across the pool.
- Hold a kickboard and walk across the pool.
- Repeat the above activities, jogging across the pool.
- Throw a ball forwards, walk (jog) to it. Repeat.
- Hold child while they flutter kick their legs in water, making as much splash as possible.
- Have child hold onto the edge of the pool and make as much splash as possible.
- Holding your child's hands, jump up and down in the water in a circle, change direction; jump forwards; jump backwards; jump from side to side.
- Repeat, but hop on one foot in the water, then the other, changing hopping foot every 4 hops.

The following ideas are for the *individual* child to ensure safety.

FIT FOCUS: STRENGTH

FIT TIP

When you move in water you are buoyant, which puts little stress on the joints of your body.

- Holding child in the water have child do the front crawl stroke; breaststroke; backstroke; treading water.
- Push a beach ball down into the water and make it 'bob' up!
- Hand paddle on a small floating board.

FIT FOCUS: FLEXIBILITY

- Holding the child face upwards in the water, let them make a wide floating shape ('star').
- Hanging onto the edge, have child lean away, stretching out as much as possible; gently open and close legs.
- Standing in water, gently push the water by slow-motion treading.
- Make up your own water stretch.

Fit Session 6

1. *Shadow dodging game*
   Partners stand one behind the other in a free space. Front partner is the 'dodger'; other partner is the 'shadow'. On your 'Go!' signal, 'shadow' tries to follow 'dodger' as close as possible as the dodger moves around the play area making quick changes of direction. On 'Freeze!' both come to a jump-stop immediately. If the shadow can touch the dodger by taking a giant pivot step towards their partner (one foot must stay in contact with the floor), then the two change roles. Have children move using different locomotion movements: walking, running, skipping, hopping, slide-stepping. Praise good stops!

2. *Chasey*
   Decide who is 'it' and how 'it' will tag free players. (Suggest pulling a flag from the back of the shorts, touching a player with a soft ball or throwing a beanbag to hit a player below the knees.) When 'it' makes the tag, players change roles and the game continues.
   VARIATION
   Have more than one 'it'.

3. *What's the time, Mr. Wolf?*
   Have children stand at the end of a marked out play area. Each time the children ask: 'What's the time, Mr. Wolf?' answer by giving a specific time such as '3 o'clock'. Children must then take 3 giant steps towards you. When you answer 'Dinnertime!', give chase trying to tag children before they safely cross over their end line. Anyone caught must join Mr. Wolf in catching others!

'3 o'clock!'

MR. WOLF

1. *Bridges and tunnels*
   Partners, with one partner making a bridge by taking weight on hands and feet, while the other partner moves through the tunnel. Then reverse roles. Explore different ways of doing this.

2. *Leapfrog*

    Partner 1 takes up a low position on all fours, tucking head down. Partner 2 'leapfrogs' over back of partner 1 to land in the same position. Partner 1 again leapfrogs over partner 2. Continue along in this way. How many leapfrogs will it take to move from one sideline to the opposite sideline?

3. *Ski jumps*

    Stand face-to-face with your partner on one side of a line. Jump together from side to side.

FIT FOCUS: FLEXIBILITY

1. *'Thread the needle'*

    From stand tall position with fingers interlocked in front of you, lean over and try to put one leg through, then the other leg. Now reverse to your start position. Remember to keep your fingers interlocked throughout this activity!

2. *'Tick-tock'*

    Stand back-to-back with child and interlock fingers. Gently lean to one side, bending knees and touch pointer finger to the ground ('tick'). Straighten, then lean to other side to do the same ('tock').

THREAD THE NEEDLE

TICK-TOCK

Fit Session 7—rope activities

FIT FOCUS: AEROBIC

13

Rope jumping activities

For short rope activities, select a rope length for each child so that when the child steps into the centre of the rope, the handles come just under arms, but no higher than the top of the shoulders.

1. *Rope patterns*

    Lay rope straight along the ground and have children jump in a zig-zag pathway from one end to the other.
    • Jump from side to side
    • Be a 'tightrope walker' along the rope

- Make a circle with your rope and the child's, then play a game of 'circle tag' around the rope
- Leap over the circle rope in different ways
- Run and take off on one foot, to land on both feet in the circle

2. *Long rope jumping*
    Using a long rope, with one end tied to a fence or post, have children take turns to stand in the centre and swing rope gently under feet. Cue children when to 'jump–jump–jump!'

- As rope jumping ability improves, challenge child to keep jumping for as long as possible
- Jump and turn around
- Jump opening and closing feet
- Jump and clap hands or snap fingers
- Jump and bounce a ball. What other challenges can you do?
- Run in 'front door' to jump in centre of rope and run out
- Gradually increase speed and duration

3. *Short rope jumping*
    Once children have developed good rhythm jumping in a long rope, use a short rope.

- Make up jumping jingles
- Hot pepper—how many jumps can be made in 30 seconds; 45 seconds; 1 minute?

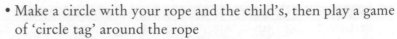

FIT FOCUS: STRENGTH

Rope circling
Hold handles of rope together in one hand. Try the following activities with one hand, then the other.

- **HELICOPTERS**
  Circle rope overhead. Can you make it 'sing'?
- **PROPELLERS**
  Circle rope in front of you. Make it sing.
- **WHEELIES**
  Circle rope with your right hand on right side; switch to your left hand and circle rope on left side.
- **TWISTERS**
  Circle rope in front of you in a figure-8 pattern.
- **STRONG HANDS**
  Fold rope in half and then in half again. Holding firmly onto ends try to pull rope apart for a 10-second count.

FIT FOCUS: FLEXIBILITY

1. Double rope and, holding it taut, stretch from side to side.

2. Double rope twice and 'thread the needle' by holding rope out in front as you step one foot through, then the other. Then step feet back out.

3. In back-lying position, put doubled rope around one foot, raise leg in air and gently pull leg towards you for 20 seconds. Repeat with other leg.

Fit Session 8

FIT FOCUS: AEROBIC/AGILITY

Use markers, such as cones, that are easily visible and set up a variety of agility courses. Here are some suggestions. Together with the children create more agility courses.

1. *Triangle run*
   Set the markers in a triangle pattern, spaced 6 metres/yards apart and marked 1, 2 and 3. Have child start at marker 1, run around marker 2, back around marker 1, then around marker 3, back around marker 1. Repeat this circuit twice.

2. *Four-leaf clover run*
   Similar set-up to Triangle run (above). See diagram below. Number markers 1, 2, 3 and 4.

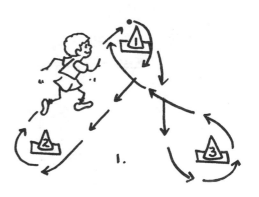

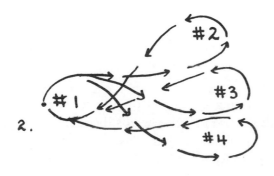

3. *Garbage collection time*

Using hoops or small ropes and beanbags, set up a row of 'garbage bins' (a beanbag in a hoop), spaced 3 metres/yards apart, in front of a starting line. Have child run to first bin, pick up beanbag, run back to starting line to place beanbag behind line. Then run to other bins in turn, until all the 'garbage' has been collected. Time how long this takes. Repeat activity by putting the garbage out again.

FIT FOCUS: STRENGTH

The following 2 activities strengthen tummy muscles.

1. *Rope climbers*

In sitting position, knees raised with weight on heels, lean back and pretend to climb a rope, hand over hand.

2. *Heel tappers*

Take weight on your hands and lean back, extend feet out to tap heels in front; then bring legs in to tap heels in close to you.

This activity strengthens leg muscles.

3. *Wall sit*

Have child lean with back flat against a wall, then slowly slide down wall until knees are bent at right angles and hold position. Have a conversation with child as they hold this position for 20 seconds. Give encouragement.

FIT FOCUS: FLEXIBILITY

1. *Knee-hug stretch*

Sitting against wall, raise one bent leg upwards clasp it and gently press towards you for 10 seconds. Change legs and repeat.

2. *Calf stretch*

Have child stand facing a wall and then lean forwards to take weight on hands. Step one leg forwards, bending at the knees. Keeping back leg straight, press the heel of back foot to floor. Hold for 10 seconds. Repeat with other leg.

Fit Session 9—out and about

FIT FOCUS: AEROBIC/AGILITY

The family outing
Just going for a 20–30 minutes walk, cycle, swim, skate, and so on with the family is a valuable socially rewarding activity, because it provides the opportunity for the entire family to share the same exercise goal, while interacting socially. Also, this will strongly reinforce the concept of fitness for life where the child can see that fitness is a family affair that can be shared and enjoyed by all!

- **WALK** with your child and dog around the neighbourhood block, park or beach. Do this together at least once a week. Set a reasonable distance and gradually increase the distance (time); but remember that children only have little legs so there is a limit to the speed at which you can walk. Walk and talk about a favourite subject. Remember to bring a water bottle along with you.
- **HIKE OR BUSH WALK** together in the park, forest, bush, state or national park. Make it a half- or full-day event and finish with a picnic!

FIT FOCUS: STRENGTH

1. *Tree push-ups*
   After completing your walk, find a tree (or similar place), lean forwards with hands flat against tree, and bend and strengthen arms to push away from tree. Repeat several times.

2. *Mountain sprinters*
   Take weight on hands and feet in a front support position, with one leg forwards, the other leg back. Exchange leg positions 10 times.

3. *Stump step-ups*
   Find a stump or similar place where you can step up and step down. How many step-ups can you do in 30 seconds?

FIT FOCUS: FLEXIBILITY

1. *Faces*
   How many different ways can you make faces? Now give me a big smile to relax the muscles in your face. Try these sounds: 'Cooo . . . eeee!' 'Aaahh!' 'Ooohh!' 'Eeehh!'

2. *Shoulder stretch*
   Stand tall and reach one hand behind your head and the other hand behind your back. Can you grab the fingers of your hands and hold in this position for at least 10 seconds? Reverse hands and do stretch again.

3. *Sprinter stretch*
   Begin on all fours. Move one leg forwards until the knee of the front leg is directly over the ankle and the other leg is extended back. Hold stretch for 10 seconds. Then gently push knee of back leg towards floor. Repeat with other leg.

Fit Session 10

16

FIT FOCUS: AEROBIC/RHYTHM

Moving to music (rhythm) can be a lifelong very enjoyable and social activity. Let child select a favourite song to play on your tape/CD player. Have your child move to the music as you give the following signals:
- Clap hands while marching on the spot
- Jog in place, snapping fingers
- Bounce on the spot in different ways
- Skip around the room
- Join hands and circle one way; circle the other way
- Link elbows and turn one way; turn the other way
- Do the 'twist'
- 'Free dancing' to the music!

FIT FOCUS: STRENGTH

1. *Hitchhike walk*
   Child stands on your feet as you walk around the room. Child gives instructions on how to move: 5 steps forwards, 8 steps

backwards; 3 steps to the right, and so on. Walk your child to the bedroom and say goodnight!

2. *Inverted hitchhiker*
   As for 'hitchhike walk' except that child is upside down, facing you, while you support legs.

3. *Create a hitchhiker dance* in this position.

FIT FOCUS: FLEXIBILITY

1. *'Wake up fingers'*
   • Slowly open and close your fingers, 'waking' them up!
   • Spider push-ups—press palms of hands together and push fingers away.
   • Long sit and 'walk your fingers' (use pointer and tall fingers) along your legs towards your toes.

2. *'Finger stretcher'*
   In stand tall position, interlock the fingers of both hands, then gently straighten your arms pushing the palms of your hands outwards. Hold this stretch for 5–10 seconds; relax.
   • Stretch in this position with arms overhead.
   • Stretch one arm out with fingers upwards. Use your other hand to push gently against these fingers. Reverse and repeat.

3. *'Foot artist'*
   In sitting position, lean back on hands for support. Lift one leg and draw circles in the air with your pointed toes. Now draw circles in the opposite direction. Repeat using the other foot.
   • Draw waves; figure-8s
   • Bring your foot in and out; up and down
   • Trace your favourite number; your initials; the word FIT

Fit Session 11

1. *Beat the challenge*

   Children partner up and stand side-by-side with inside feet touching. Each pair takes note of its home spot. A challenge is given. Each partner tries to get the task completed and return to the home spot before the other partner.

   CHALLENGES
   - Touch the 2 end lines with 2 hands and return home
   - Touch the sidelines with one hand and one foot; return home
   - Touch 2 cone markers on each boundary line and return home
   - Touch each corner of the rectangular play area with one foot and return home
   - Jump over 10 different ropes or objects (such as soft toys) and return home

   VARIATION
   Score 1 point each time for being the first partner to complete the challenge. First partner to return home has the other partner do 3 of something.

'DEAD BUG'

2. *Frozen tag*

   Select 3 'its' who each have a tagging object. On signal 'Tag!', 'its' try to tag free players. Any player tagged by an 'it' is immediately frozen (decide on a 'frozen' shape, such as a 'dead bug' or wide shape). After about 30 seconds select 3 of the 'frozen' players to be the new 'its' and start a new game.

   VARIATION
   Have 'its' pull flags to capture a player.

1. *Wheelbarrow*

   Partner 1 stands behind partner 2 who is on all fours in front of the standing partner. Partner 1 gently holds partner 2 by the upper leg so that partner 2 takes weight on hands. Now partner 2 tries to walk hands across the floor. Emphasise that partner 2 does not arch back!

2. *Stubborn mule*

   Take up same position as for wheelbarrow. 'Driver' tries to move ahead, but 'mule' won't budge.

3. *Stubborn driver*

   'Mule' tries to walk hands forwards, but 'driver' won't budge.

DRIVER   MULE

FIT FOCUS: FLEXIBILITY

1. *Mirrors*
   Use relaxing background music. Partners face each other and slowly move stretching limbs in different directions. Partner 1 copies partner 2's movements, then both switch roles.

2. *Puppets*
   One partner is the 'puppet' and gets into back-lying position; the other partner is the puppeteer who pulls the 'strings' to lift different body parts. Puppet responds with each string pull.

FIT TIP

Establish a focus word such as PRIDE
'P'—be Positive
'R'—be Respectful
'I'—Intelligent decisions (make good choices)
'D'—Dream, be Determined
'E'—be Enthusiastic!

Fit Session 12—miming, acting and dancing

18

FIT FOCUS: AEROBIC

1. Create an action poem and do the actions together. Pretend we are going swimming: front crawl, back crawl, breaststroke, tread water, butterfly, dog paddle.

2. Mime movements such as:
   • Climbing a ladder
   • Rollerblading or ice-skating (figure skating)
   • Hiking up a mountain
   • Trekking through a jungle
   • Landing on the moon and taking a moon walk
   • Cheerleading
   • Conducting an orchestra

3. Play commercial dances for children and together perform the dancing actions, such as 'Looby loo', 'Birdy dance'.

4. Act out movements for classic fairy tales such as:
   • 'Jack and the Beanstalk'
   • 'The Three Little Pigs'
   • 'Little Red Riding Hood'

FIT TIP

Children love to be creative. Encourage and provide opportunities for them to express their imaginations through movement.

FIT FOCUS: STRENGTH

Animal walk dance
Create an animal walk 'dance' using animal walks such as:
- Puppy dog—walk on all fours
- Camel—right limbs move, then left
- Kangaroo jump—jumping with feet together
- Bunny hop—hands move out, then feet follow
- Snail—sitting position, slide bottom along floor using legs; hands support back

FIT FOCUS: FLEXIBILITY

1. *Shakers*
   Start with one body part shake; then shake 2 parts; then 3 parts; then 4 parts; 5 parts; 6 parts; all over.

2. *Rockers*
   From sitting position, feet together and cross-legged, rock forwards and backwards; from side to side; rock up to standing position and stretch high.

3. *Rollers*
   Stretch out on your front and, keeping this long pencil shape, roll in one direction; then other direction.

Fit Session 13

19

FIT FOCUS: AEROBIC/RHYTHM

A rebounder is a mini-trampoline that can be purchased from a variety of retail stores. Rebound activities are ideal for those days when the weather is not suitable to be outside and also provide variety in an exercise program. Ensure that the rebounder is located in a safe area, away from any obstacles. Teach children to enjoy and, at the same time, respect the equipment in a safe way! Using music while child is moving on rebounder will enhance rhythm.

Movements
- Side strides (feet together, feet apart)
- Front strides (alternating front and back feet)
- Jogging in circle to right; to left
- Jumping, keeping knees high
- Ski jumping from side to side, feet together
- Jumping while crossing one foot in front of the other; then behind the other
- Jumping to slap heels behind; heels in front
- Your turn to create a 'rebound' movement!

FIT FOCUS: STRENGTH/ALERTNESS

Partner up with someone who is about the same size.

1. *Leg wrestling*
   Both lie on your backs in opposite directions, hip to hip and interlock legs at the ankle. On signal 'Go!' try to push each other's leg to the ground.

2. *Arm wrestling*
   Lie on fronts facing each other and position right arms at right angles, supporting on the upper arm. Use your other arm to support you as well. Interlock fingers and try to push the other person's hand to the floor.

Who will be the wrestling champ for the day? [For the wrestling activities slowly increase the level of resistance and let the child have a 'win' now and then.]

1. LEG WRESTLING

2. ARM WRESTLING

FIT FOCUS: FLEXIBILITY

1. *Flagpole*
   Lean back and onto one side, then grab the top leg with the hand on that side. Stretch leg into the air and hold for 5–10 seconds. Then repeat with other leg and hand.

> **FIT TIP**
>
> Pain is no gain. Listen to your body. Stretch within your comfortable range of movement.

2. *Cross-leg hug*
   'Dead bug!' wiggle-wiggle-wiggle. Now cross your legs and hold each foot, hugging legs close to body for a 10-second count. Feel the stretch in your seat muscles. Cross legs the opposite way and hug legs close to body for another 10 seconds.

Fit Session 14

20

FIT FOCUS: AEROBIC/ALERTNESS

Dodging games are popular with all ages and provide great cardiovascular, agility, alertness and spatial benefits, besides being good fun! Here are examples of simple dodging games that can be played with 2, 3 or more players. Emphasise always knowing where the ball is coming from, watching out for others and playing fairly.

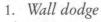

1. *Wall dodge*
   Mark out a space near a wall area in which the game is to be played. The child must stay in this space. Roll a large soft ball towards the child at a speed they can handle. Children love to think you are trying to trick them, so baulk, turn your back on them and suddenly spin around; gently throw. Switch roles after a while.

2. *Dodger in the middle*
   If 3 people play: 2 rollers or throwers and 1 'dodger' in the middle. 4 people: 2 rollers and 2 dodgers.

3. *Team dodgeball*
   Divide a large group of children into 2 even teams. One team stands inside a large marked circle with a 6 metre/yard diameter; other team stands around the outside of the circle, evenly spacing themselves. Circle players roll a large playground ball towards the inside players, trying to hit them below the knees. Once a player has been hit, that player must join the circle team and fetch balls for the circle players to roll. The circle team is given a certain time to try to 'capture' as many of the inside players as possible; then the teams switch roles and play is continued.

4. Invent a dodging game of your own!

FIT FOCUS: STRENGTH

1. *Crab push-ups*
   Take up a crab-walk position on all fours, face up. Remove one arm to tap your bottom, return to place, then repeat with other arm. Continue in this way for as long as you can.

2. *Finger push-ups*
   Take up a position on all fours, face down. Lean forwards to take weight on hands. Push up onto fingers, then flatten. Continue in this way for as long as you can.

FIT FOCUS: FLEXIBILITY

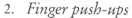

1. *Knee huggers*
   Stretch out flat on your back along floor, then bring both legs up and hold at ankles for 10 seconds. Then bend knees and hug to chest. Hold this position for another 10 seconds. Stretch to back-lying position. Repeat 2 more times.

> **FIT TIP**
> Always remind your child to bend from the hips and not from the neck.

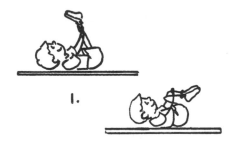

2. *Butterfly stretch*
   In sitting position, with soles of feet touching, gently push down with elbows on the inside of the knee area for 10 seconds. Relax pressure, then repeat 2 more times.

Fit Session 15

FIT FOCUS: AEROBIC/ALERTNESS

Flag chase
Flags are very useful as a method of 'safe' tagging in chasey-type games. They can be inexpensively made by cutting polyester material into 50 cm × 6 cm (20 in × 2½ in) strips. Flags are then tucked into the back of the children's shorts or pants. Check that each child has about two-thirds of the flag showing.

- Play simple flag chase with the child
- Play partner flag chase
- Select 3 or 4 'its' and play flag chase. Change 'its' after a certain time
- Play team flag chase

FIT FOCUS: STRENGTH

Water bottle shakers
Fill small water bottles with sand, some half full and some completely full. Children hold a water bottle in each hand and do the following activities.

- Shake-shake-shake in front, above head, to each side, behind back
- Shake-shake-shake in a full body circle
- Shake apart; shake close together
- Shake high; shake low
- Move bottles up and down, up and down
- Move bottles forwards and backwards
- Move bottles out and in, out and in
- Punch with the water bottles
- Slash with the water bottles
- **BODY BUILDERS**
  Pretend that you are body builders. What different muscle poses can you do?

FIT FOCUS: FLEXIBILITY

Under and over stretching
Partners stand back-to-back to start, then reach under and between legs and touch hands.
VARIATIONS
- Reach above the head and touch hands
- Twist to the left slowly and smoothly touch hands
- Repeat to the right
- Pass a water bottle to each other

Fit Session 16

22

FIT FOCUS: AEROBIC/ALERTNESS

1. *Balance tag*
   Select one or more children to be 'it' depending on the number of children involved. A player is in the 'safe' position from being tagged by performing a balance (stork stand). Have children practise this safe balance before playing this game. After a certain time, select a new 'it' and a new 'safe' balance and play the game again.

2. *Island tag*
   Mark out several 2 metres/yards diameter circles (using rope) or chalk in a 15 metres/15 yards square play area. These are 'islands'. Select 1 or 2 children to be sharks. Children must try to 'swim' from one island to another without getting tagged by the 'great white sharks' (you or 2 'its'). An island is a safe spot, but only for a 5-second count—then you must leave it.
   VARIATION
   Use non-slip carpet squares as the 'islands'.

FIT FOCUS: STRENGTH

1. Use non-slip carpet squares as the 'islands'. Set up different patterns with the squares and go 'island hopping' (jumping from one square to another!).

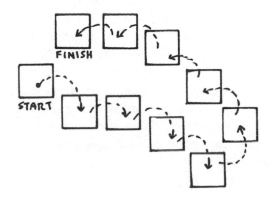

BOUNCING BALL

SCOOTERS

ROCKING CHAIR

BEAR HUG

FLAMINGO

FIT TIP

Balances are more stable if the base of the support is wider.

2. *Partner strengthening stunts*

- **BOUNCING BALL**
  One partner is the ball; the other partner is the ball bouncer.
- **SCOOTERS**
  In a sitting position facing your child, hook feet under each other's bottoms. Try to move forwards.
- **ROCKING CHAIR**
  In same position as for 'scooters', try to rock each other. (You will have to help your child 'lift' you!)

FIT FOCUS: FLEXIBILITY

1. *Bear hug*
   Standing tall, lift one knee and hug it to your chest. Repeat with the other knee.

2. *Flamingo stretch*
   You may need to support children or have them hold onto a table, chair, fence, etc. while they balance on one foot and grasp the ankle of the other foot. Have children gently pull the foot up to touch the buttocks. Hold for 10 seconds. Repeat with other foot.

Fit Session 17

23

FIT FOCUS: AEROBIC/ALERTNESS

Balloon play

Balloons are excellent for developing manipulative, hand–eye coordination and tracking skills, besides just being a whole lot of fun and providing beneficial fitness activity. Balloons, like floating scarves, move in slow motion and are therefore easy for young children to track. Balloons are inexpensive and come in a variety of colours, sizes and shapes. For younger children, start with a bigger round balloon, then gradually reduce the size of the balloon as skill level improves. Ideally, have a balloon for each child. Use a marking pen to write name on each child's balloon. Ensure that the play area is free of any obstacles that could hinder play. Also commercially available are 'balloon balls' which have washable cloth balloon covers that make fragile normal balloons much more durable and wearable. The balloon is simply inserted through a small slit in the cover, inflated and then can be hit, punched or kicked.

Balloon activities

1. Keep your balloon up using different body parts. How many different body parts can you use?

2. Use one hand, then the other to hit the balloon. Keep this order going. Repeat with different fingers.

3. Keep the balloon up in the air using a right body part, then a left body part. Keep alternating right and left body parts in this way.

4. Call out the body part to be used to tap the balloon: right pointer finger; left foot; right shoulder; left elbow; right knee; head. Try combinations such as: head and knee; elbow and foot; head–knee–foot.

5. Pretend you are a soccer player and use only your head, knees or feet.

6. Pretend you are a tennis player and bat the balloon with your open hand. Use one hand, then the other.

7. Now keep the balloon up in the air like a volleyball player. Interlock your fingers and keeping arms straight hit the balloon with your forearms.

8. Have partners try to keep up one balloon between them, using different body parts; use a right body part, then a left body part.

9. Stretch a long rope across two high chairs or between two poles.
   • Play 'balloon volleyball'
   • Play 'balloon tennis'

10. Invent a balloon game of your own and play it with a friend!

FIT FOCUS: STRENGTH

For these activities use a large balloon or a medium-sized beach ball.

1. *Balloon pick-up*
   Lie on your tummies, facing each other with a balloon placed between you. Using only your heads and working together, slowly lift balloon to the standing position.

2. *Cooperative balloon travel*
Explore different ways of travelling with your balloon using different body parts; for example, hold balloon between your backs and travel together or position balloon between your shoulders and travel.

3. *Balloon volley*
Using a large bed sheet or light plastic sheet, try to shake several balloons up and down on the sheet.

FIT FOCUS: FLEXIBILITY

1. *Pass the balloon*
Partners, back-to-back, pass the balloon overhead, between the legs; then between the legs, overhead.

2. *Over-the-top relay*
In groups of 4 or 5, one behind the other, pass the balloon over the top to the end player, who runs to the front of the line to pass the balloon.

FIT TIP

Remember to 'smile' and enjoy your play!

3. *Through-the-legs relay*
Pass the balloon between the legs.

4. *Balloon keep-up*
In groups of 4–5, players must keep the balloon from hitting the floor. Players are not allowed to hit the balloon twice in a row. Count the number of hits made in a certain time limit.

Fit Session 18

24

FIT FOCUS: AEROBIC/RHYTHM

1. *Treadmill walking* or *stepper walking* if the weather is not the best for going outdoors.

2. *Exercise to music*
   Encourage children to continue to move for the length of the song; then gradually increase the time!
   • Head: nod, shake, gently roll from side to side
   • Shoulders: shake, shrug, circle
   • Arms: swing one at a time, backwards and forwards, swing arms together; circling, opening and closing
   • Legs/feet: shaking, bending, lunging, leg lifting
   • Feet on tiptoes then flat; ankle circling; point and flex
   • Hands: fingers opening and closing; making a fist, relaxing; waving; finger snapping; hand clapping; interlocking; pulling against each other

3. Together follow a children's exercise video.

FIT FOCUS: STRENGTH

1. *Coffee grinder*
   Place one hand on the floor and run your feet around in a circle, in one direction, then the other. Repeat with the other hand.

2. *Compass*
   In front support position, walk your hands around in a circle while your feet stay in one place.

FIT FOCUS: FLEXIBILITY

1. *Shoulder shrugs*
   • Shrug your shoulders up and down
   • Roll your shoulders gently backwards; then gently forwards
   • Alternate lifting one shoulder, then the other
   • Alternate rolling your shoulders backwards

2. *Knee circles*
   Keeping your knees close together, circle your knees gently in one direction for 5 circles, then in the other.

FIT TIP

It is important to keep your ankles strong from an early age. When you are watching TV or during the commercial breaks do some ankle circles!

3. *Ankle circles*
In sitting position, circle your ankles 5 times in one direction, then circle in the other direction. Point your ankles away from each other, then point your ankles towards you (flex). Use the cue words: 'Point!', 'Flex!', 'Point!', 'Flex!'. Repeat this pattern 2 more times!

Fit Session 19

FIT FOCUS: AEROBIC/ALERTNESS

Bicycling activities

Insist that children wear bike helmets at all times while cycling. Also insist that they carry a water bottle attached to their bike or in their backpack.

1. Together with friends or parents bicycle in safe areas.

2. Tricycle or bicycle as a parent/friend walks/jogs along.

3. In an open space, such as a car park, challenge children to:
   • cycle in a straight line or along marked lines
   • cycle between markers
   • cycle around a marked rectangle

FIT TIP

Remember to be a courteous cyclist and obey the traffic rules. Always wear a bike helmet and cycle in safe areas!

4. Call out signals: 'Red light!' (stop); 'Right turn!' (signal with right hand and make turn); 'Left turn!'; 'Yellow light!' (sit on bike and practise looking both ways).

5. Bicycle in slow motion from A to B. How slow can you go?

6. Cycle along designated bicycle paths through the park, along river banks, along beach footpaths.

FIT FOCUS: STRENGTH/COORDINATION

When you get to your favourite park or open space:
• Throw a football to each other
• Throw a frisbee to each other
• Kick a soccer ball back and forth
• Shoot a basketball at a hoop
• Throw a boomerang

FIT FOCUS: FLEXIBILITY

Bicycle warm-ups/warm-downs

1. *Neck stretch*
   Stretch your neck muscles by gently dropping your head forwards and slowly moving it in a half circle to the right and then to the left.

2. *Back stretch*
   Stretch up towards the sky. Hang on a horizontal bar.

3. *Arm circles*
   Circle arms gently backwards.

4. *Wing stretchers*
   Gently open and close your arms, keeping your elbows level with your shoulders. Now squeeze your shoulder blades together and hold for 10 seconds. Relax and repeat.

5. *Leg stretcher*
   To stretch quadriceps, hip and thigh muscles, step forwards with right foot, touching left knee to floor. Keep knees bent no more than 90 degrees. Hold for 20 seconds. Repeat with other leg.

Fit Session 20—skating and hockey stick activities

Skating activities

Where necessary, purchase and insist that children (and you) wear the proper safety equipment to protect against injury. Participate with the children if you can. Offer encouragement and support to the new learner; otherwise watch and give encouraging smiles!

1. Take children ice-skating to an indoor or outdoor rink.

2. Go rollerblading along park pathways.

3. Take children roller-skating.

4. There are many games children can play while doing skating activities, such as:
    - tag-type games
    - weaving in and out of obstacles
    - starting and stopping; turns and spins
    - jumps in the air; jumps off ramps
    - create stunts of their own!

5. Hockey stick play with a partner or in a small group.

1. *Bells*
    Put the stick on the floor and stand facing it. Jump back and forth over the stick.

2. *Skiers*

Stand side-on to the stick and jump back and forth over the stick.

3. *Stick jumps*

One partner holds the stick just off the ground; the other partner jumps over it from a two-foot take-off. Gradually partner raises the stick further off the ground. Switch roles.

4. *Stick tug of war*

Partners stand on either side of a line. Partners hold the stick horizontally between them and try to pull the other partner over the line. Emphasise safety.

FIT TIP

Make fitness a family affair whenever you can!

FIT FOCUS: FLEXIBILITY

Stick stretches

Use hockey sticks or long plastic poles about the same height as the children.

FIT TIP

Work at achieving good control first, then speed after!

1. Hold the stick in your hands. Make yourself as long as the stick as you stand on your tiptoes and stretch your arms and hands as high as possible overhead.

2. Put the stick behind your back, with one hand holding it behind at the lower end, and the other hand holding it at the top end. Gently push forwards with the lower hand, to stretch the shoulder of the opposite hand. Hold for 10 seconds, then change hands.

3. Holding stick horizontally above head, gently stretch to one side and hold for 5 seconds, then to the other side. Push your belly-button out, rather than bending forwards, so that you will get a better stretch.

Fit Session 21—snow play

27

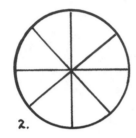

FIT FOCUS: AEROBIC/ALERTNESS

1. Make a snowman together, starting with a small snowball and rolling it into a larger and larger snowball. Create a variety of 'snow creatures' or 'ice sculptures'.

2. Make snow forts and play 'snow ball tag'. Remember that the most enjoyable play is safe play! Be considerate of others.

3. *Fox and geese tag*
   Use snow boots to mark out a large pie and cut into 8 pie shapes as shown. Fox starts in the middle and tries to capture the geese who move on the paths. A captured goose becomes the helper, or the fox and goose change roles.

FIT FOCUS: STRENGTH/COORDINATION

1. *Toboggan* together on gentle slopes.

2. *Cross-country ski* through the park trails.

FIT TIP

Always bend at your knees to pick up something from a low level, so that you don't hurt your back!

FIT FOCUS: FLEXIBILITY

1. *Ball massage*
   This should feel very soothing after an activity session in the snow. Using relaxing background music will help create a pleasant environment. Have the child lie on stomach. Roll a tennis ball over child's legs, back, arms, feet. While massaging with the ball, ask child to close eyes. Think happy thoughts and just relax.

2. Now ask them to breathe in slowly for 5 seconds; then breathe out slowly for another 5 seconds.

Your turn!

Fit Session 22

FIT FOCUS: AEROBIC/COORDINATION BALANCE

Pogo stick jumping

You may need to support children at first until they have established a good sense of balance on their pogo sticks.

• Bounce in a straight line; in a circle; in a square
• Bounce from side to side; forwards and backwards
• Make up a pogo stick dance
• Invent other ways of bouncing on your pogo stick

VARIATION

Use a LoLo™ Ball.

FIT FOCUS: STRENGTH/COORDINATION

These activities focus on developing strong tummy muscles. These tummy toners should be done on a comfortable surface, such as a mat, carpet or folded large beach towel. Show children how to breathe properly: breathing in as they curl up; breathing out as they curl down. Emphasise not to hold their breath.

1. *Peek-a-boo*
   In hook-lying position, hands at sides, curl up head to look at knees, hold, then slowly curl down. Breathe in while curling up. Breathe out while curling down.

PEEK-A-BOO

2. *Ankle tappers*
   Begin in back-lying position. Curl forwards to tap a hand to the inside of the opposite ankle. Slowly curl down to lying position. Curl back up and tap with other hand to opposite ankle. Continue in this way.

ANKLE TAPPERS

3. *Twisting sit-ups*
   Begin in back-lying position with your knees bent at 90 degrees and fingers at ears. Curl up to touch opposite knee with your elbow; curl down. Then curl back up to touch other knee with opposite elbow. Continue in this way.

TWISTING SIT-UPS

FIT FOCUS: FLEXIBILITY

Tension alert

If possible use soft background music. Have children lie on their backs and close eyes. Call out different body parts to tighten, then relax.

Tighten toes of left foot (curl toes)—relax.

Tighten toes of right foot—relax.

Tighten tops of legs—relax.

Continue with buttocks, stomach, neck, shoulders, arms, hands, fingers, jaw and eyes.

Tighten up all over!

Then let everything relax like a floppy doll!

FIT TIP

It is important to balance your play with rest.

Fit Session 23—ball play

29

FIT FOCUS: AEROBIC/QUICKNESS

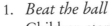

1. *Beat the ball*
   Children start at one end line of a large play area. Teacher rolls the ball from this end down towards the opposite end line. On signal 'Go!' children run to the opposite end line trying to beat the rolling ball. Emphasise safety.

2. *Agility run and roll*
   Mark off a square that is 5 × 5 metres/yards. One player stands with ball in one corner of square; the other partner stands with ball in diagonally opposite corner as shown. On signal 'Roll!' each one rolls ball down the line to the adjacent corner and then runs to receive the other partner's ball and roll it back. Continue in this way.

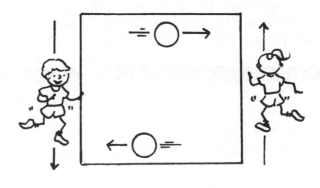

FIT FOCUS: STRENGTH/COORDINATION

FIT TIP

Fit kids have more fun than 'couch potatoes'!

Jump the ball

Children form a large circle and space themselves an arm's length apart. Teacher or parent stands in the centre and swings a jump ball (ball or throwing ring with rope attached to it) in a large circle along the ground. Children must jump over the ball without letting it touch their feet as the ball swings towards them. If the ball does contact a child's feet, then the child must run to touch a designated tree and then can rejoin the game. Swing jump ball in one direction, then after a while change direction. Gradually raise the ball off the ground, but no higher than knee height.

VARIATION

Play so that you get 2 'lives' or chances then, the third time that you are hit by the swinging ball, you are out!

FIT FOCUS: FLEXIBILITY

1. *Ball circles*

   Take ball in your hand and trace a large circle. Bend your knees as ball travels low to ground. Circle 3 times in one direction; then 3 times in the other.

2. *Ball leg roll*

   In sitting position, legs together and stretched out, roll ball from your lap right to your toes, keeping your legs straight. Hold ball on your toes. Stretch ball overhead in lying position and repeat leg roll. Do this 3 times.

Fit Session 24—hoop play

30

Hoop play

Hoops can be purchased at a toy store and provide hours of inexpensive fun.

SLIDE-STEP

1. *Traffic lights*

   Have children colour in 3 large circles each drawn on a piece of thick cardboard: 1 green circle, 1 red and 1 yellow. Mark off a large rectangular area. Have children step inside their hoop and hold it at waist height. This is their car and the different coloured circles are the traffic lights.

   'Green!'—run quickly anywhere in the play area

   'Red!'—freeze immediately, then jog in place

   'Yellow!'—use another way of moving, such as skipping, jumping, marching—but move slowly and carefully!

2. *Traffic lights*

   You may need to initially start rolling the hoop for young children, but encourage and teach the children to get the hoop rolling for themselves.

   • Roll your hoop along the ground and run after it to catch it in front of you.
   • Roll your hoop and carefully dive through it.
   • Roll hoop back and forth to each other.
   • Raise and lower hoop overhead and then in front. Continue this pattern for 8 times.
   • Jump in and out of your hoop with both feet; then with one foot.
   • Skip with your hoop as if it was a jump rope.

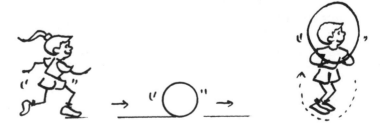

FIT FOCUS: STRENGTH/COORDINATION

Hoop jump
Children place hoop on the floor. Check for good spacing. Start inside the hoop.
- Jump out to the front, jump inside
- Jump out to the back, jump inside
- Jump out to one side, jump inside
- Jump out to other side, jump inside
- Jump in and out of hoop
- Keep feet in hoop and walk hands around it
- Children form groups of 5–6 and place hoops in a pattern as shown. They take turns jumping through the hoops from start to finish. Create a new hoop jumping pattern.

FIT FOCUS: FLEXIBILITY

1. Show me how you can make your hoop turn around your waist (doing the 'hula-hula').

2. Hold your hoop horizontally as you stretch to one side and hold, then to the other side.

3. Hold the hoop in front of you and let your eyes trace its shape in one direction, then in the other.

FIT TIP

Good physical fitness can help you to move safely and to meet unexpected emergencies.

Fit Session 25

FIT FOCUS: AEROBIC/AGILITY

1. *Sock attack*
    Set a certain time limit (2 minutes). Partners place 2 hoops about 10 metres/yards apart and place 5 beanbags or rolled up socks in each of the hoops. To start, each partner stands in one hoop. On signal 'Sock attack!' each partner picks up a sock from their hoop and runs to place it in the other partner's hoop.

Continue in this way until time is up. The object is to have the least number of socks in your hoop.

2. *Box the stocking*

Suspend a ball in a sock or stocking from a clothes line or tree. The ball needs to hang about children's chest height. Have children take turns to 'box' the stocking while moving on the spot for 'bouts' of 30 seconds. You could even provide a commentary on the action which the children will probably enjoy listening to as they box away. Have children practise 'dancing' footwork as they throw right and left punches into the air.

FIT FOCUS: STRENGTH/BALANCE

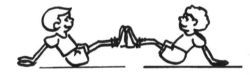

1. *Body push*

Partners about the same size face each other and touch palm-to-palm (arms straight). On the count of 1-2-3, partners try to push each other backwards.

CHALLENGE

Try to do this while standing on one foot!

2. *Foot push*

Partners about the same size face each other in the sitting position, with the soles of the feet touching. Now try to push against the other's feet.

FIT FOCUS: FLEXIBILITY

Mirrors

Use relaxing background music if possible. Partners facing and contacting palm-to-palm, mirror movements, such as slow arm circles; raising hands upwards; sideways; downwards.

Other suggestions: body circles; leg lunges. Take turns being the leader.

Neighbourhood activities

1. *Trampoline play*

   If you have a trampoline in your back yard or access to one in another way, the trampoline can be used to strengthen leg muscles, as well as improve aerobic capacity. Emphasise that the child stay in the centre on the trampoline, do a safety jump to stop movement, allow only one child on the trampoline at a time, and get off carefully. The trampoline should have safety pads around all the sides. Mark an 'X' in the centre of the trampoline with chalk. Ensure that each child takes little 'stretching breaks', as this is quite a strenuous activity.

   TRAMPOLINE ACTIVITIES

   * Do little bounces up and down on the 'X' spot, bending at the knees. Look straight ahead and make circles with your arms as you jump upwards.
   * Bounce while clapping your hands; snapping your fingers.
   * Stop by bending at your knees, feet shoulder-width apart and arms held sideways for balance.
   * Bounce again, gradually see how high you can bounce.
   * Bounce and turn in a circle, one direction, other direction.
   * Bounce down on your knees and back up to your feet.
   * Bounce onto your seat and back up to your feet.
   * Can you bounce from knees, to seat, to feet?
   * Bounce with feet together, feet apart; bounce changing front foot.

   MORE TRAMPOLINE CHALLENGES

   * Do quarter jump-turns (90-degree turns); half jump-turns(180 degrees); three-quarter jump-turns; full turns (360 degrees).
   * Have child bounce on the trampoline while catching a ball and throwing it back to you; skip with a short rope.
   * Bounce on trampoline while tossing and catching a ball.

FIT TIP

In choosing the location for the trampoline, ensure that there are no dangerous objects near it.

• Bounce to touch toes in front; bounce to touch heels behind you.
• What other stunts can you do?
• Lie down on the trampoline and stretch out wide and hold for 10 seconds; curl up into a ball and stay for a 10-second count; with your feet in the air grasp your ankles and hold for 10 seconds.

2. *Family walks*

WALKING THE DOG/NEIGHBOURHOOD WALK

Walk with the children and dog around the neighbourhood block, park or beach. Do this together at least once a week. Set a reasonable distance and gradually increase the distance (time); but remember that children only have little legs so there is a limit to the speed at which you can walk. Walk and talk about a favourite subject. Remember to bring a water bottle along with you.

HIKE OR BUSH WALK together in the park, forest, bush, state or national park. Make it a half- or full-day event and finish with a picnic!

THE 'VITE!' WALK

This is not your usual way of walking! The family lines up one behind the other to start and then all continue to walk at the same pace, keeping in order, except for the last family member who walks faster or jogs to get to the front of the line. When they take over as the new leader, they call out 'Vite!' (French for 'go quickly'). This is the signal for the last family member to follow pursuit. Decide how many 'Vite' you want to achieve on this walk, and on the next walk strive for more! Now try to pick up the tempo and have all family members jog along at a comfortable pace.

VARIATION

Space family members 1 metre/yard apart and have back runner zig-zag run to the front of the file.

3. *Hopscotch*

   This is an old favourite and is a great coordination/leg strength activity for children of all ages. Together design a hopscotch pattern using chalk on the tarmac or brightly coloured floor tape on tiles. A pattern is illustrated. With smaller children, the hopscotch spaces will need to be closer together. Use a soft throwing item, such as a beanbag. Together make up the rules of your game ensuring that the children will experience success. Cognitive variations may include using letters, shapes or colours instead of numbers.

   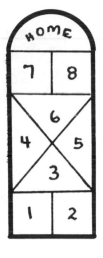

4. *Playground equipment fun*

   Playgrounds offer a variety of equipment to develop overall strength and agility, coordination and balance. Swing on different swings, climb up and slide down, hand walk across a horizontal ladder, glide across on a flying fox, crawl through a tunnel, move on a climbing net, climb up, down, over, under and through the monkey bars, climb up and over a wooden trestle, hang from a horizontal bar or ring, balance walk along a beam, slide down the pole.

Park or school oval activities

33

1. *Kite flying*
   Take children to a large open space, playground area or sports oval, void of any electrical wires. Of course, you will need a windy day for flying kites! Children could make their own kites as a project, rather than purchasing commercial ones.

2. *Frisbee golf*
   Recommend that the 'ring' type frisbee be used for young children (easier to throw). Together with the children create and mark out a 'golf course' in your neighbourhood park or school oval using trees, posts and other objects as the 'holes'. Pick your 'tee-off' spot. See illustration.

   RULES
   • Throw frisbee until target ('hole') is hit.
   • Count the number of throws taken to hit the target.
   • Record the score on a scorecard and add up your scores at the end.

   VARIATIONS
   • Create a 'par' for each hole and discuss with the children how to achieve a 'par' for that particular hole.
   • Use other objects to throw, such as beanbags.
   • **SOCCER GOLF**
   Set up a similar course, but use a soccer ball which is kicked towards target until it is hit.

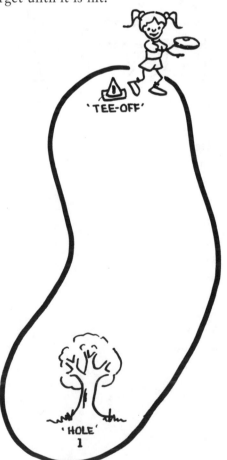

'TEE-OFF'

'HOLE'
1

3. *Tyre roll play*

    Pick up a tyre from a spare parts yard.
    *   Roll it down a gently sloping area. Give chase.
    *   Roll the tyre back up the hill.
    *   Roll it so that it changes direction.
    *   Roll it and run around it.
    *   Can you roll it and safely dive through it?
    *   Show me other tricks you can do with your tyre.
    *   Roll the tyre back and forth to each other. Stop it first to get control before rolling it back.
    *   Make a bridge over the tyre.
    *   Make a bridge on the tyre.
    *   Hook your feet under the tyre and, keeping your knees bent, do 20 sit-ups.
    *   Jump your feet in and out of the tyre.

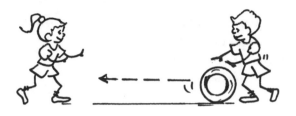

4. *Socktail play*

    Place a tennis ball or rolled up socks in an old stocking or long football or basketball sock to make a 'socktail'. Knot the stocking at the top of the ball. A commercial product called a 'Foxtail' can be purchased from most toy stores.

    Together try the following activities:
    *   Gripping the tail of the stocking, swing it around and around in a large forward arc, and let it go high as possible into the air. Try to catch the socktail as it comes down. How high can your socktail go?
    *   Swing your socktail and let it go and up to see how far you can get your socktail to travel. Then run and fetch it.
    *   Swing your socktail and send it back and forth to each other.
    *   Overhand throw socktail to each other by grasping the head of the socktail and throwing it.
    *   Send the socktail back and forth over a low net.

    SOCKTAIL VOLLEYBALL

    Play with the whole family, using 2–4 socktails and a volleyball court with a 2 metres/yards net height. Divide the family members into 2 even teams who face each other on opposite sides of the net. Each team has 2 socktails and throws them over the net into the opposition's court. The object of the game is to catch the socktail so that it doesn't land on your side of the net; otherwise the other team scores a 'socktail point'. Appoint someone on each team to keep score.

Seasonal activities

34

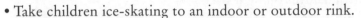

Skating fun

Where necessary, insist that children (and you) wear the proper safety equipment to protect against injury. Participate with the children if you can. Offer encouragement and support to the new learner; otherwise watch and give encouraging smiles!

- Take children ice-skating to an indoor or outdoor rink.
- Go rollerblading along park pathways.
- Take children roller-skating.
- There are many games children can play while doing skating activities, such as:
  - 'chasey-tag' games
  - hockey stick play
  - weaving in and out of obstacles
  - starting and stopping; turns and spins
  - jumps in the air; jumps off ramps
  - create stunts of their own!

Wintertime fun

- Make a snowman together, starting with a small snowball and rolling it into a larger and larger snowball. Create a variety of 'snow creatures' or 'ice sculptures'.
- Make snow forts and play 'snowball tag'. Remember that the most enjoyable play is safe play. Be considerate of others.
- Toboggan together on gentle slopes.
- Cross-country ski through the park trails.
- Downhill ski at local slopes.

Pool fun

DIVING RINGS

These can be purchased from your local pool store or toy store. Scatter rings into the water at a suitable depth for children, and have children dive down to retrieve rings one at a time. Offer praise and encouragement for their efforts!

FLOATING RINGS

These are large hoop-like rings which will float in the water. Choose the following tasks according to the ability level of the children.
- Swim through rings
- Jump into ring from the edge of the pool
- Swim through 3 rings spaced 1 metre/yard apart
- Hold a ring vertically in the water and have child dive from edge of pool through ring
- Invent your own ring game!

POOL TAG

You are allowed to come out of the pool if being chased by another swimmer, then re-enter somewhere else.

Beach fun
- At the beach, walk through knee-deep water
- Run through knee-deep water
- Throw a frisbee or tennis ball to each other in the water
- Jump over waves
- Quickly run away so the waves can't catch you
- Dig a large hole or make a sandcastle together
- Boogie board
- Stretch out to the corners of your large beach towel
- Roll up towel and stretch it behind your back; then stretch from one side to the other side
- Make a 'sand angel' by lying on your back and opening and closing your arms and legs

'SAND ANGEL'

> **FIT TIP**
>
> Remember to wear sunscreen and a hat for protection against the sun's harmful UV rays: 'Slip-Slop-Slap!'

Rainy day/Limited space activities

1. *Individual activities*

   ### 'LET'S PRETEND YOU ARE A . . .'
   (Remember to watch where you are going!)
   - 747 jet taking off down the runway, lift off and then fly!
   - lawn-mower cutting the grass
   - jet ski slicing through the water
   - hawk swooping down on a small animal
   - hockey player scoring a goal
   - figure skater spinning
   - shadow-boxer punching into the air and 'dancing' with your feet

35

• a karate kid kicking with your feet and slashing with your hands
• a hummingbird flitting from flower to flower
• a prancing horse
• a snake wriggling along the ground

2. *Animal walks*
Begin in your home space. Show me how you can move like the following animals:
• Crab—walk on all fours face upwards.
• Kangaroo—jumping, with hands held up in front.
• Puppy dog—walk on all fours.
• Bunny hop—all fours, with hands moving forwards first, then feet. Continue in this way.
• Seal—move along using your forearms and dragging your feet behind you as you move along.
• Inchworm crawl—begin in front support position (on hands and feet, facing downwards). Walk hands away from feet, then walk feet up to hands. Continue to 'inch' along in this way!
• Bucking bronco—take your weight on your hands and kick your legs gently up into the air. How high can your legs go!
• Animal walk—make up your own animal walk!

3. *'Do this, do that'*
In this activity the child copies your movement which can be strength, agility, flexibility, cardiovascular, balance, coordination, power . . . When you say 'Do this!' the child copies you. When you say 'Do that!', they must not move. Make the changes quickly.

4. *Let's play 'touch!'*
• Touch a cone marker or a sideline with your right knee
• Touch a cone on an end line with your left foot and right hand
• Run to the other sideline and touch a cone with your head
• Run to the opposite end line and touch a cone with your right elbow and left knee
• Go 'Home!' and 'corkscrew' with left arms and legs crossed
• Sink your corkscrew to cross-leg sit. Now try to stand tall

5. *Balance feathers*
    Each child takes a balance feather to their home space and
    quietly explores balancing the feather:
    - in the palm of the hand
    - back of the hand, each finger
    - one hand, other hand
    - other body parts, such as elbows, shoulders, knees, head
    - moving from standing to sitting position and back up to
      standing
    - transferring feather from palm of one hand to palm of the
      other
    - transferring feather from back of one hand to back of the other.

    VARIATION
    Challenge children to transfer one balance feather from one
    partner to the other, using different body parts! Use thin,
    lightweight 'staking sticks'.

6. *Rope circling*
    Hold handles of rope together in one hand. Try the following
    activities with one hand, then the other.

    - **HELICOPTERS**
      Circle rope overhead. Can you make it 'sing'?

    - **PROPELLERS**
      Circle rope in front of you. Make it sing.

    - **WHEELIES**
      Circle rope with your right hand on right side; switch to your
      left hand and circle rope on left side.

    - **TWISTERS**
      Circle rope in front in a figure-8 pattern.

    - **ROPE YANK**
      Fold rope in half and then again in half. Holding firmly onto
      ends try to pull rope apart for a 10-second count.

7. *Rope jumping activities*
    For short rope activities, size the rope for children by having
    them step into the centre of the rope then check that the
    handles come just under arms, but no higher than the top of the
    shoulders.

• **JUMPING PATTERNS**

Lay rope straight along the ground and have child jump in a zig-zag pathway from one end to the other. Jump from side to side. Then be a 'tightrope walker' along the rope. Make a circle with your rope and your child's. Play a game of 'circle tag' around the rope. Leap over the circle rope in different ways. Run and take off on one foot, land with both feet in the circle.

• **LONG ROPE JUMPING**

Using a long rope, with one end tied to a fence or post, have child stand in the centre and swing rope gently under their feet. Cue child when to jump, 'Jump–jump–jump!' As rope jumping ability improves, challenge child to keep jumping for as long as possible. Jump and turn around; jump opening and closing feet; jump and clap hands or snap fingers; jump and bounce a ball. What other challenges can you do? Run in 'front door' to jump in centre of rope and run out. Gradually increase speed and duration.

• **SHORT ROPE JUMPING**

Once children have developed good rhythm jumping in a long rope, then use a short rope.
  • Make up jumping jingles
  • Hot pepper—how many jumps can be made in 30 seconds; 45 seconds; 1 minute?

Limited space ideas for small and large group activities

36

Partner activities

1. *'Pockets'*

    In partners, move in and out of each other's shapes, filling in the empty spaces. For example, the first partner forms a shape; second partner forms a shape around the first partner by filling in the empty space created by the first partner's shape. First partner then moves to form a shape around the second partner. Continue in this way. Encourage 'flowing' movements.

2. *Leapfrog*
    Find a partner and leapfrog from sideline to sideline. Leapfrog
    by placing hands on partner's back and straddle-jumping over
    partner.

3. *Follow-the-leader*
    Find a partner and stand together in a home space one behind
    the other. Take turns being the leader and the follower, changing
    on my whistle signal. Think of lots of different ways that you
    can move. How many different body parts can you warm up?

4. *Dog and bone*
    This agility game is best played with 2 children. Mark off 2 lines
    that are 8 m (25 ft) apart and place a hoop equal distance
    between the lines. In the hoop place a beanbag or small ball.
    Have each child stand just behind their line, facing the hoop.
    On signal 'Bone!' both children run quickly towards hoop to
    see which one can get there first to 'steal' the bone and take it
    back to their 'home' line before being caught by the other 'dog'.
    Have children get into different starting positions and watch
    the fun! Each player was a flag tucked into back of the shorts so
    that ⅔'s of the flag is showing. The flag is pulled to make the
    catch.

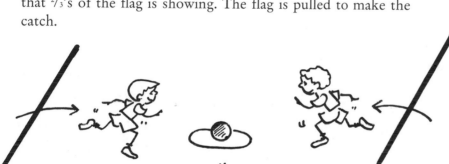

5. *Beanbag horseshoes*
    Children partner off, each collecting 2 beanbags and one
    throwing ring for the pair. Partners then find a free space and
    place the ring 3 metres/yards from a throwing line. Each partner
    tosses their beanbag towards the throwing ring. Adjust distance
    to suit the skill level of the children. Play to 5 points. Challenge
    another player.

6. *Wall bounce*
    Partners stand near a wall, facing it. Partners, in turn, toss a ball
    at the wall and the other tries to catch it after one bounce off
    the ground. Offer challenges such as 'clap' hands before
    catching the ball; 'snap' fingers; 'touch' your shoulders; turn
    around once.

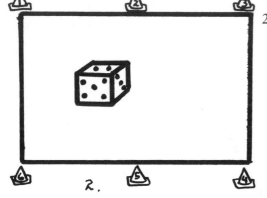

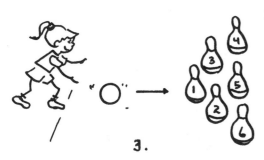

Small and large group activities

1. *Barnyard chatter*

   Name each team after farm animals, such as pigs, cows, ducks, chickens, sheep and have each animal find a home space. Ask each team to practise the sound of its animal; for example, pigs 'oink'; cows 'moo'. On signal 'Barnyard chatter!' close your eyes, put your hands up in front of you as bumpers and carefully walk around making the sound of your animal. When you find someone who sounds like you, hold hands, and continue to listen for and find other members of your team. Which team can collect its members the quickest and cross-leg sit in a circle? Remember no peeking—play fair!

   VARIATION

   Use another theme such as the colours of the rainbow—red, orange, yellow, green, blue, indigo and violet.

2. *Lucky corner*

   Use markers positioned at 6 locations in a large rectangular area or hexagonal shape. With a marking pen, number the markers 1–6 as shown in the diagram. On signal 'Corner!' players run to a location of their choice and stay there jogging on the spot. Throw a large die and see which number comes up. Players caught in the corner with that number must come to the centre of the play area and do stretches; the other players continue the game. When only 6 players remain, each player must run to a different location! Who will be the last player?

3. *Bowling fun*

   Using 6 pins or plastic bottles set up in a 'V' formation children try to knock over the pins or bottles by rolling a small playground ball at them. Each bowler get 2 tries and counts the number of pins or bottles knocked over to earn a score. Keep track of score and add up the scores after 3 turns to get a total. Play this activity in pairs or groups of 3–4, 2 bowlers, 2 players to reset the pins.

4. *Dodger in the middle*

   Play with 3–4 children: 2 rollers or throwers and 1 or 2 'dodgers' in the middle. If a roller hits a dodger, then both change places.

5. *Changing motions*
   Have everyone long-sit in a big circle facing the centre. Ask children to follow your motions as you clap your hands, tap your feet, nod your head, and so on. Now tell them that they will have a turn at being leader, except for one player who will step out of the circle and stand with back to the rest of the class. This player is 'it' and must try to guess within 3 goes who the leader is. Secretly choose one of the children to be the leader. This leader must change the movements without 'it' being able to detect what is happening.

Integrated activities

1. *Traffic lights*
   Have children colour in 3 large circles each drawn on a piece of thick cardboard: 1 green circle, 1 red and 1 yellow. Mark off a large rectangular area. Have children step inside their hoop and hold it at waist height. This is their car and the different coloured circles are the traffic lights.
   • 'Green!'—run quickly anywhere in the play area
   • 'Red!'—freeze immediately, then jog in place
   • 'Yellow!'—use another way of moving, such as skipping, jumping, marching—but move slowly and carefully!
   Children learn colour identification and visual response. This activity also provides a good opportunity to teach road safety.
   VARIATION:
   Use traffic signs: octagon—Stop; triangle—Give way; roundabout—Give right of way on a roundabout.

2. *Beanbag bucket toss*

Suggest setting up 3 mini-stations. For each station use 6 ice cream containers or buckets labelled red, orange, yellow, green, blue and purple; and one set of beanbags in these rainbow colours. If possible, use double-sided tape to secure the buckets to the floor so they won't move. Players can decide how they want to arrange the buckets. Players pair off and take turns to toss 6 beanbags into the corresponding bucket, keeping track of successes. Rotate to each mini-station. Vary the tossing distances. Children learn colour association (and number or shape association in the variations), hand–eye coordination, accuracy tossing and cooperation.

VARIATIONS

- Vary how the buckets are positioned: on the floor; on a chair; on a bench.
- Use dominant hand to throw 3 beanbags; non-dominant hand to throw 3.
- Numbered beanbags and numbered containers.
- Shape beanbags with the corresponding shape on each container.

3. *Beanbag shuffleboard*

Use floor tape to mark off a 4 × 3 metres/yards grid or use an ink marker to draw grid onto a large plastic sheet or poster board as shown. Mark in the squares the letter corresponding to the 6 rainbow colours: red (R), orange (O), yellow (Y), green (G), blue (B) and purple (P). Have players pair off and stand on one of the four sides of the grid. Each pair has a set of rainbow coloured beanbags. Each partner gets 3 beanbags to slide or toss into the corresponding colour on the grid. Score 2 points for beanbag completely landing inside the colour square; 1 point if touching the correct grid area. Round 1 score; round 2 score; round 3 score, and so on. Play for 7 rounds, then challenge a new partner. Children learn maths concepts of addition, colour association and accuracy tossing.

VARIATION

Give each grid square a number value from 1–6. Number the beanbags from 1–6.

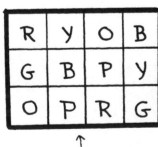

4. *Beanbag target toss*

   Place scattered numbered squares as shown. Players toss beanbags onto numbered squares (or spots) and earn the points shown on the face of the square. Add up scores after 6 throws to get a total.

   VARIATION

   Everyone starts with 100 points and subtracts scores from this total. Object is to get the lowest score in a certain number of throws.

5. *Dice-ercise*

   Purchase large dice at toy shops or educational sports catalogue companies. Children jog CCW around an oval track marked out with dome cones. Teacher rolls the die in the centre of the play area:

   1—power walk CW once around the play area
   2—jump rope for 2 minutes
   3—touch the middle of 3 walls slide-stepping
   4—do 4 push-ups in each corner of play area
   5—do 5 sit-ups on each of the boundary lines
   6—slide-step across from sideline to sideline 6 times

6. *Colours-n-dots*

   Each face of the die has a different colour and a different set of dots from 1 to 6. Mark out a large rectangular play area. Scatter dome cones throughout—one for each player. Players start game by standing near a dome cone. Both dice are rolled. Players perform the activity, then return to their home marker. Primary colours are red, blue and yellow; secondary colours are green, orange and purple.

   Red (both red)—sprint to the opposite end line and back
   Blue (both blue)—jump back and forth along an end line
   Yellow (both yellow)—leap over cones scattered in play area
   Green (blue/yellow)—hop across the play area
   Orange (red/yellow)—slide-step to the opposite side line and back
   Purple (red/blue)—jog to touch each of the 4 corners with one hand/one foot

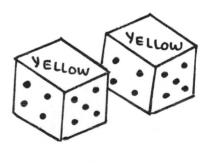

LEAPFROG

BACK-TO BACK
GET-UP

VARIATION

Count the number of dots face up on the dice.
• For an odd sum, sprint to the opposite end line and back.
• For an even sum, leap over the cones scattered in the play area.
• For a double, do 'jump turns' on the spot.

7. *Vegie–fruit die play*
Write the names of 3 vegetables and 3 fruits on the 6 faces of each die. One die is rolled at a time. Create an activity or exercise associated with each vegetable or fruit. Examples follow:
Corn—wring the dishrag with a partner
Carrot—bucking bronco
Broccoli—snake roll with a partner
Strawberry—back-to-back get-up
Pear—thread the needle
Orange—leapfrog with a partner
Other vegies: peas, beans, lettuce or spinach
Other fruits: bananas, apples, grapes

VARIATION

Draw the vegetables and fruits on the dice with different vegetables and fruits showing on each die.

8. *Dice maths relay—multiplication—2 to 6 times tables*
Players cross-leg sit in teams of 4 at one end of the play area. Teacher rolls 2 dice in the centre of the play area. First player of each team runs to the middle to observe numbers on dice, then runs to opposite end to write answer on a whiteboard in designated box as shown. Score 1 point for the correct answer. Score another point for being the first one to do so. Teacher quickly records the score. Then dice are thrown again. After everyone has gone twice, a team dice maths champ is determined!

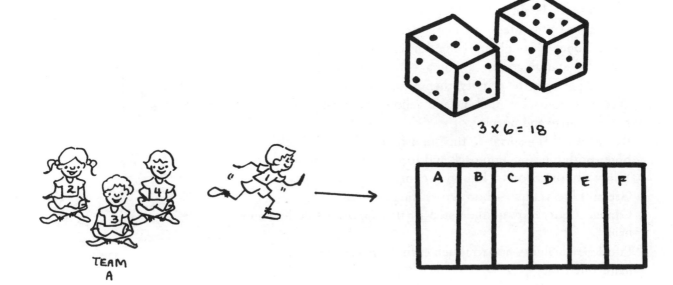

$3 \times 6 = 18$

TEAM A

A	B	C	D	E	F

9. *Alphabet scramble run*

Use marking pens to create a set of alphabet cones. Spread alphabet cones throughout a large play area. Beside each cone place a plastic container with 30 counters (for example, 30 letter A). The letter on the counter corresponds to the letter on the cone. To start, each runner stands beside one of the lettered cones. On signal 'Alphabet run!' each runner must collect a set of all the alphabet counters and place them into a plastic bag. At the completion of this, runners find a home space to spread out counters in alphabetical order. If you are missing a letter, you will need to run back to that alphabet cone and collect the counter there! The challenge is to do this the quickest! Remember, play fairly!

VARIATIONS

• Runners must collect the counters in alphabetical order!

• Instead of collecting a counter, have runners collect a maths card.

When all 26 cards have been collected, each player must write down the answers for each of the 26 maths cards. Include addition, subtraction, multiplication, division and fraction work questions appropriate for the ability level of the children.

10. *Alphabet orienteering*

Use marking pens to create a set of numbered cones. Spread 15–20 numbered cones throughout a large play area. Give each pair a 'directional map' showing the path of the cones to be followed and a plastic bag. At each 'checkpoint' each pair of runners collects one alphabet stick with a letter written on it (will need 15–20 alphabet sticks at each checkpoint). Runners must complete the course in order until all the numbered cones have been visited and alphabet sticks collected. At the finish each pair then finds a station square and together use alphabet sticks to create as many words as possible!

CHECK POINT #1

VARIATIONS

• Instead of alphabet sticks, create maths sticks with multiplication and division questions (or simple equations for older groups), suitable for the ability level of the class.

• Declare overall orienteering partner champs!

11. *Alphabet exercise circuit*

Set up an exercise circuit using alphabet cones to establish order: number cones to indicate the repetition for each exercise and station squares to display the instructions.
Some examples follow:
Alphabet cone A, Number cone 10—push-ups
Alphabet cone B, Number cone 20—tummy crunchers
Alphabet cone C, Number cone 1—1 minute jump rope
Alphabet cone D, Number cone 8—8 step-ups
Alphabet cone E, Number cone 4—run to touch 4 lines

VARIATIONS

Change the numbered cone at certain stations to increase the fitness demands. For example, Alphabet cone C, Numbered cone 2: 2 minute jump rope.

12. *Beanbag golf*

Set up 6 golf holes as shown using carpet squares or small hoops as the 'holes'. Number cones as the flag markers and use small cones or dome cones as the tee-off markers as shown. If possible correspond each hole with number and colour. For example, hole number 1 has a red tee-off marker and a red flag marker. Assign three players to a hole, with each player tossing an alphabet beanbag. Count the number of tosses taken to land their beanbag in the hole. Record score on a beanbag golf card as shown.

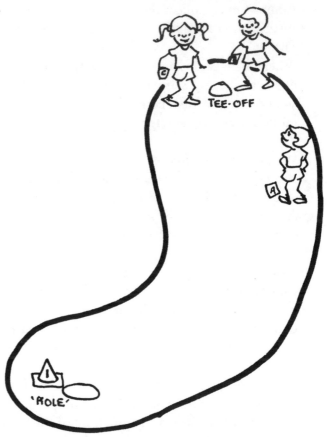

BEANBAG GOLF SCORE CARD			
PLAYER			
HOLE	1	2	3
#1			
#2			
#3			
#4			
#5			
#6			
TOTAL			

13. *Maths-ercise*

Create or purchase a pack of jumbo playing cards.
Let the 'face' cards represent the different maths operations:
Ace—multiplication   King—division
Queen—addition   Jack—subtraction
Jokers—zero   All the other cards are face value
Form teams of 6. Each team starts at one end of the play area. Separate the cards into face cards and numbered cards. Draw a face card and 2 numbered cards. The first player of each team must determine the outcome and quickly run to the opposite end of the gym to write the answer on a whiteboard before the other players can, to score a point for their team. Then the next

player goes. This is a team effort, so everyone can help to determine the answer. 'Is this your final answer?' Determine a winning team after round 1, then play round 2. Continue in this way.

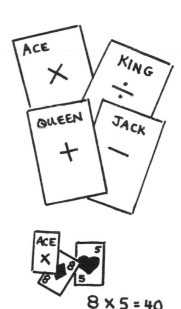

14. *'Let's run around Australia!'*

Use the map shown with the different 'dots' marked off. Each time the children move aerobically for a continuous 3 minutes (Level 1), 5 minutes (Level 2) and 8 minutes (Level 3), colour in a dot. Learn about Australia as the children travel from state to state! For example, start from Perth and travel east across the countryside. When you get to Kalgoorlie, study gold mining. As you progress around learn about the deserts, Uluru (Ayers Rock) at Alice Springs, Barossa Valley, Tasmania, the Blue Mountains and the Great Barrier Reef. Learn about the native animals of Australia. Don't forget to watch out for kangaroos along the way!

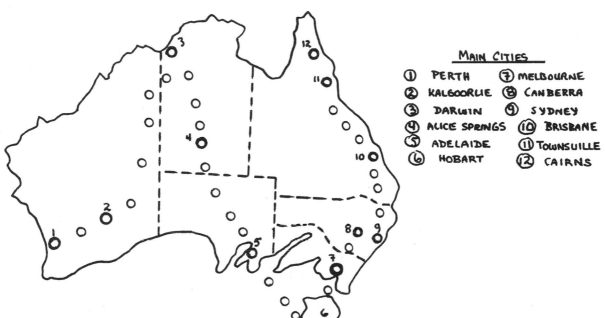

Chasey-type activities

1. *Simple chasey*

Decide who is 'it' and how 'it' will tag you. (Suggest pulling a flag from the back of the children's shorts, touching them with a soft ball or throwing a beanbag to hit them below their knees.) When 'it' makes the tag, you become 'it' and give chase.

2. *Frozen tag*

Select three 'its' who each have a tagging object. On signal 'Tag!' 'its' try to tag free players. Any player tagged by an 'it' is immediately frozen. (Decide on a frozen shape, such as a 'dead bug' or wide shape.) After a certain time, change the 'its' and start a new game.

VARIATION

Have 'its' pull flags to capture a player.

3. *Stingers*

Mark out or designate a large rectangular area. Pair up children. One partner is number 1; the other partner is number 2. Number 1s hold 'stingers' (beanbag, soft ball or soft object) and on signal 'Stingers!' give chase to their partners. If 1 stings 2 by tagging them with the object, then 2 becomes the stinger. Continue in this way. Remind players to watch where they are going and to stay inside the play area.

VARIATIONS

- It player is allowed to throw the object at partner, but object must make contact below the knees.
- Half the children are stinger bees with small soft objects. They give chase to the other half, throwing the objects to sting them below the knees. If stung, the tagged player becomes a 'helper bee' and fetches the object for the stinger bee. Eventually all the players will be caught. Change roles and play the game again.

4. *Partner tag*

Children pair up, stand side-by-side and join inside hands. Two pairs are selected to be the 'it' pairs and each partner of the 'it' pair holds a tagging object in their outside hands. On a signal 'its' give chase. A free pair who has been tagged must join the 'it' team. Gradually the 'it' team will get bigger and bigger, until there are only a few free pairs left.

5. 'Chain tag'

Select 3 players as the 'its'. Once a player is tagged, that player must join onto 'it'. Players in chain must keep their inside hands joined and use only outside hands to make the tag. Two chains can decide to link up together. Watch the action as each chain grows in size! Remind chain players that they must keep their handholds.

VARIATION

Once a chain gets to 6 players the chain can break-off into 2 chains of 3.

6. 'Pirate tag!'

Stand at one end of the ship. Choose 3 players to be the 'pirates' who stand in the middle of the ship. On signal 'Pirates are coming!' all other players must try to cross the ship without being tagged. If tagged, that player is 'frozen' to the spot, but may use arms to touch other players crossing and thus be set free. After a while, choose new pirates and continue the game.

Use soft objects or pull flags to make the tag.

Low-organised games

39

1. *Heads, tails and pockets*
   Have children get into groups of 3. In each group designate one person to be a 'head' who places preferred hand on head; a 'tail' who places preferred hand on bottom; and a 'pocket' who places preferred hand in pocket. On signal 'Tag!', 'heads', 'tails' and 'pockets' try to tag each other, transforming the tagged player to look like the tagger. In the beginning there will be equal numbers in each group. On signal 'Freeze!' the game stops (or use music to start and stop the game). Now count the numbers in each group and make a comparison with the numbers at the beginning of the game. Play game again!

2. *Octopus*
   Mark out a large rectangular play area which is the 'ocean'. The free players, or 'fish', start at one end of the play area. Choose an octopus who is 'it'. The octopus stands in the centre and gives the signal 'Swim fish, swim!' for the fish to try to 'swim through the ocean' (run across the play area) to the opposite end line without getting tagged by the Octopus, who uses a soft object such as a beanbag or soft ball to make the tag. A tagged fish becomes a 'tentacle' and must sink to the floor in knee-sit position. This player is only allowed to use hands to tag other fish as they run pass. If successful, the tagger becomes a fish again and the tagged player becomes a tentacle. Change the Octopus after a while and begin a new game. Emphasise that players always watch where they are going!
   VARIATIONS
   • Have 2–3 Octopuses.
   • Pull a flag to catch a fish.
   • Have fish start at both ends of the play area, creating two-way traffic.

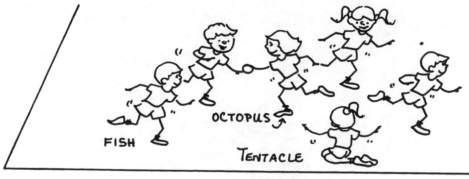

THE OCEAN
2.

3. *Partner flag tag*

Make flags by cutting strips of polyester material into 50 cm × 6 cm (20 ins × 2½ ins) strips. Have children tuck flags into the back of their shorts or pants, then pair off and number '1' or '2'. Call out either '1' or '2'. This is the signal for that partner to try to tag the other partner by pulling their flag. The challenge is to try to pull the partner's flag before another number is called. Remind players to watch where they are going at all times. Play fairly!

VARIATION

Vary the way the players can move: brisk walking, jogging, skipping, slide-stepping.

4. *Tail snatch*

Each player has a tail tucked in at the back of their shorts. Make sure that two-thirds of the tail is showing. On signal 'Tail snatch!' players try to snatch other players' tails without getting their own snatched away. Snatched tails must be held in one hand while the other hand is used to capture other tails. A player whose tail has been snatched away is still in the game. On signal 'Freeze!' the game stops immediately. Each player counts the number of tails they have, including their own if it was not captured. Declare a 'Tail snatch champ' and play again.

5. *Team tail snatch*

Each team is given a certain coloured tail to tuck into the back of each player's shorts: red team, green team, blue team and yellow team. On signal 'Red!' the red team is the 'it' team and must try to capture as many of the other teams' tails as they can in a certain time limit (say 20 seconds). A player whose tail has been captured must jog in place. When the 'Freeze!' signal is given, everyone stops the game. Red team quickly counts up the number of tails captured. Tails are returned to the respective players. Players wait for the next colour signal to be given. Which team can capture the most number of tails? Emphasise watching where you are going at all times! Play fairly!

6. *Hickory, dickory dock*

Mark out a circle (about 4 metres/yards diameter) in a large rectangular play area. Parent/teacher stands in the middle. Children position around the outside of the circle and move in a CW (or CCW direction) singing the rhyme: 'Hickory, dickory dock, the mouse ran up the clock. The clock struck one, the mouse ran down, Hickory, dickory dock.' The mice (children) then ask 'Where is the cat?' The teacher can give different responses (sleeping, playing, eating . . .) each time the mice ask the question. But when the teacher answers with 'Chasing!' this is the signal for the mice to quickly scamper to the safety of their hole (outside the rectangular area) before they get caught. Any mice captured must join the cat in helping to catch other mice. To make the game safer, use flags tucked into the back of the shorts.

6.

Large group activities

40

1. *Family dodge ball*

Mark off a large circle using rope or other markers. Have half the family members stand inside the circle, the other half space themselves evenly around the circle. Use a large ball to roll or throw at circle members. If you are successful at hitting a member below the knees, you get to take that person's place in the circle.

'PIRATE'

2. *Flag pirates*

Select three players to be the 'Pirates!' and have them stand in the centre of the play area. Everyone else has a flag tucked into the back of their shorts. When a pirate pulls the flag, the two players exchange roles. Emphasise that players watch where they are going at all times.

VARIATION

Use a beanbag or soft ball to make the tag.

3. *Team colours tag*

This tagging game requires a large open space and 4–6 sets of flags (red, blue, yellow, green, orange). Divide the group into 4 or 5 even teams of 5–6 players, depending upon the number of players. Each team is assigned a colour: group 1—red; group 2—blue; group 3—yellow; group 4—green; group 5—orange and given a corresponding set of flags. Players must tuck the flag into the back of their shorts so that three-quarters of the flag is showing. Check this. Now have everyone scatter in the open play area. On your signal 'Red!' (name a colour), the red team is the 'it' team and has exactly 20 seconds to try to capture as many flags from the other players as possible. If a player's flag is pulled, then that player must jog on the spot. At the end of 20 seconds, blow a whistle to stop play. Count the number of 'caught players' and record the red team's score. Continue in this way until each team has had a turn at being the 'it' team. At the end determine the best tagging team of the day! Emphasise that players keep their heads up to avoid collisions. The game is a strenuous one—the players will need a rest after this!

4. *Team leapfrog*

Teams of 4–5 position in file formation behind a listening line. Check for good spacing. Leapfrog by placing hands gently on the back of the player in front (who is curled up on all fours, keeping head down) and straddle-jump over this player. Last 'frog' at the back begins the race by 'leapfrogging' over the backs of each member in front. Once you reach the front, squat down and call out 'Ribbet!' which is the signal for the next frog to go. Which team will be the first to get all its frogs across the opposite end line?

5. *Protected person*

This is a family activity. Have all but one child join hands and form a circle. The object of the game is for the tagger (child) to quickly run around the outside of the circle and try to tag a nominated person (Mum). The circle moves in such a way as to protect the nominated person from the tagger. Give the tagger a certain time to tag the circle player; then have the nominated circle player step out and nominate another circle player to try to tag. Continue the activity in this way. Remind tagging players that they are not allowed to reach inside the circle to try to make the tag.

VARIATION

IKE, MIKE, SQUEAK AND WILBER

For each group of 4 players, name one player 'Ike', a second player 'Mike', a third player 'Squeak' and the fourth player 'Wilber.' Have the 'Squeaks' step outside of the circle and select a circle player who they will try to tag (Wilbers). Play activity as above.

6. *Lucky corner*

Use markers positioned at 6 locations in a large rectangular area or hexagonal shape. With a marking pen, number the markers 1–6 as shown. On signal 'Corner!' players must run as quickly and carefully as they can to stand in one of the 6 locations and stay there jogging in place. Throw a large die and see which number comes up. Players caught in the location with that number must come to the centre of the play area and do stretches; the other players continue the game. When only 6 players remain, each player must run to a different location! Who will be the last 2 players?

7. *Jump the ball*

Children form a large circle and space themselves an arm's length apart. Teacher or parent stands in the centre and swings a jump ball (ball or throwing ring with rope attached to it) in a large circle along the ground. Children must jump over the ball without letting it touch their feet as the ball swings towards them. If the ball does contact a child's feet, then the child must run to touch a designated tree and then can rejoin the game. Swing jump ball in one direction, then after a while change direction. Gradually raise the ball off the ground, but no higher than knee height.

VARIATION

Play so that you get 2 'lives' or chances, then the third time that you are hit by the swinging ball, you are out.

Parachute play

1. *Shake, shake, shake*

Children space evenly around the parachute, gripping handles or the seam with an underhand grip. Spread the parachute out at waist height and slowly, gently, quietly begin to shake the parachute. Gradually increase from ripples, to mini-waves, to rolling waves, to surf's up, to king waves!

2. *Body waves*

Lower the parachute to the ground and on signal 'Up!' raise the parachute overhead letting it billow with air, then slowly bring it all the way down. Repeat 2–3 times.

BODY WAVES

3. *Mushroom*

   Inflate the parachute on signal '1-2-3, up!' walk into centre 3 steps then, on signal 'Down!', lower parachute sealing seam to the ground and making a mushroom shape.

4. *Igloo*

   Grip the parachute with right hand over left. Inflate the parachute again, take 3 steps towards centre of parachute, then pull the parachute behind you, uncrossing your arms and cross-leg sit on it to seal in the air. Who lives in 'igloos'?

IGLOO

5. *Merry-go-round (carousel)*

   Hold onto the parachute with right hand, everyone facing in a CW direction. Use cue words such as walk, power walk, jog. On whistle, players quickly switch to travel in the opposite direction. Keep parachute stretched out and have players gently raise and lower parachute as they travel. Hold parachute with both hands, and slide-step CW/CCW, gently shaking the parachute.

MERRY-GO-ROUND

6. *Fireman's pull*

   Face parachute and stretch it out using an overhand grip. Glue feet to the floor and carefully lean back keeping parachute taut. Hold for 10 seconds.

7. *Wild horses pull*

   Turn back to parachute and grip with underhand grip. Try to pull parachute away from its centre. Feel the stretch in your arms and legs.

8. *Chook and critter tag*

Place a chook (rubber chicken) and a beanbag critter in the middle of the parachute. Children use an overhand grip to shake the parachute. Challenge is to see which critter will tag the other first! Watch the fun as the children will shake until their arms are ready to drop off!

CHOOK & CRITTER TAG

9. *Popcorn*

Place several beanbags in the centre of a parachute held at waist height. Challenge is to see how quickly beanbags can be 'popped' or shaken off the parachute.

10. *Mission impossible*

Number the players 1–2, 1–2 around the parachute. Place several beanbag critters in the centre of the parachute. Have 1s take one giant step away from the parachute. On signal 'Shake!' 2s' challenge is to try to shake all the critters off the parachute. 1s' challenge is to catch, or fetch, the beanbag critters and toss them back on the parachute. Watch the fun! Switch roles and play again.

MISSION IMPOSSIBLE!

11. *Wrist roll*

Holding parachute at waist level, palms-down grip, children gently roll the parachute towards the centre. Emphasise keeping the parachute taut. Ask children if they can feel their wrists tighten up as they continue to roll up the parachute. When the parachute is almost completely rolled up, have children gently drop the parachute to the ground and step away, so that it can be collected and put away.

Large group party activities

1. *Tap heads*

   Have children find a home spot and cross-leg sit, then rest their heads on their hands and close eyes as shown. Ask them to think of something very pleasant like playing at the beach on a warm sunny day. Shhhhh . . . be quiet. Now walk around the room and gently tap children on the head. Each child tapped quietly gets up and follows behind the leader, joining the end of the line. Who will be the last one to be tapped? (The birthday boy or girl!) Wake up the birthday boy or girl and sing 'Happy Birthday to you!' Finish with 3 'Hip-hip-hoorays!'

2. *Tall to small*

   Divide the children into even teams of about 6. Have teams scatter throughout the play area and do a 'Scrambled eggs— walk!' (walk in and out of each other without touching). On signal 'Tall to small!' each team must carefully but quickly find its members and arrange itself to stand from tallest to smallest.
   • Do again, but this time, give the signal 'Small to tall!'
   • Repeat, and have teams arrange themselves alphabetically, using first names.
   • Arrange themselves by birthdays!
   • Combine the teams and play game again.
   • Try this as a whole group activity and watch the fun!

3. *Changing motions*

   Have everyone long-sit in a big circle facing the centre. Ask children to follow your motions as you clap your hands, tap your feet, nod your head, and so on. Now tell them that they will have a turn at being leader, except for one player who will step out of the circle and stand with back to the rest of the class. This player is 'it' and must try to guess within 3 goes who the leader is. Secretly choose one of the children to be the leader. This leader must change the movements without 'it' being able to detect what is happening.

4. *Balloon play*

    • **BALLOON KEEP-UP**

    Groups of 4–5 players must keep a large balloon or balloon ball from hitting the floor. Players are not allowed to hit the balloon twice in a row. Count the number of hits made in a certain time limit.

Balloon keep-up

• **BALLOON POP**

Use string to tie a balloon to each child's ankle. Then challenge children to try to 'pop' the balloon by stepping on it! (Some children may be frightened by the noise of the balloons popping, therefore don't force them to do this activity!)

Balloon pop

• **COOPERATIVE BALLOON TRAVEL**

Explore different ways of travelling with your balloon using different body parts; for example, hold balloon between your backs and travel together; position balloon between your shoulders and travel.

Balloon travel

• **BALLOON IN SPACE**

One half of the party group forms a circle around the other half, who lie on the floor in 'dead bug' position. Launch (toss) a large balloon into the middle. The object is to keep the balloon airborne! The standing group and the lying down group work together to accomplish the task at hand (feet, too)! After a certain time or if the balloon contacts the ground, the groups switch.

Balloon in space

5. *Guard the nest*

    Mark out a large play area. Select one player to be the 'Eagle' who stands on one end line of the play area and guards the 'nest' (end line); the other players start on the opposite end line. Eagle turns their back to the players and begins counting to 5 out loud. Players begin to sneak towards the Eagle, who quickly turns to face the oncoming players and gives the 'eagle-eye' to try to catch anyone moving. Players must stay very alert and freeze immediately before the Eagle turns around. A player caught moving must fly back to the start line. First player to cross the Eagle's end line becomes the new Eagle and the game begins again.

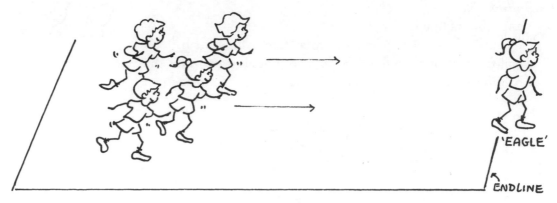

6. *Worm grab*

For each game, form 2 equal teams of 6–8 players and arrange the teams in 2 lines about 6 m (20 ft) apart, standing and facing each other. For a large group, set up 2 games and conduct them simultaneously. Give each team a bird's name, such as Galahs, Magpies, Cockatoos and Kookaburras. Have player 'birds' from each team number off: 1, 2, 3, 4, 5, 6. Place a hoop, the 'nest', in the middle between the lines and in the nest place 2 ropes, the 'worms', or soft objects (such as rubber rings, beanbags). Call out a number, for example, '3'! The two players with that number run to the hoop. Each grabs a 'worm' and then returns with it to their line. The player who does this the quickest earns a point for the team. Now add another 2 worms to the nest and call out another number. When all players have had a turn, each team counts the number of worms collected. Team with the most worms is the best 'bird team' for the day!

7. *For other large group party activities refer to:*
   • What's the time Mr Wolf?—page 80
   • Barnyard chatter—page 122
   • Octopus—page 132

Cooperative activities

1. *'Gotcha!'*
   Everyone sits in a large circle in cross-leg sit position quite near to the person on either side and with right thumb up and left hand flat and over the thumb of the person on your left. (See illustration.) Wait for my signal 'Gotcha!' It may be heard when you least expect so. Then on signal 'Gotcha!' try to grab the thumb of the person on your left while, at the same time, trying to pull your own thumb away from being caught.
   - Repeat with your eyes closed. Listen carefully for the signal.
   - Reverse so that left thumb is up; right hand is flat over the thumb of the person on your right.
   - Again repeat with eyes closed.

1.

2. *Shrinking islands*
   You will need enough carpet squares, hoops or ropes so that initially there is one carpet square per player. These are the 'islands'. Players move around the squares to the music. In the meantime you remove 2–3 carpets. When the music stops everyone must jump onto a carpet square, but now some players will have to share. Continue removing the carpet squares until there are only a few 'islands' left to share. Watch the fun!

2.

3. *The limbo*
   This activity involves coordination and balance, and good flexibility, particularly of the back area. Use suitable music, such as Chubby Checker's 'Limbo Rock' available through music stores. Each team has its own limbo corner. Check for good spacing. Two dancers hold a long pole (PVC piping) or stretch a rope between them starting at waist height. Dancers take turns 'limboing' under the pole or rope: keep belly-button upwards, do not let hands touch the floor and move with a 2-feet shuffle

3.

under the rope. Feet will go first, head last! Gradually lower the pole. Who in your team will limbo the lowest? Challenge another group. Have a class challenge and declare a boy and girl limbo champs.

4.   *Charades*
Divide the children into teams of 4–5 and have each team sit together in a certain area. Players in each team then number off 1, 2, 3, 4, 5. Write on small index cards the names of several animals, birds, objects and place into a large container. On signal 'Charades!' the number 1 players run to the container and pick out a card. They quickly run to their team and act out the name on the selected card. When the name is correctly guessed, number 2 players run to the container to draw a card. Continue in this way for a certain time. The object of the game is for each team to guess as many names as possible before the time is up! Who will be the Charade champs at the end of the game?

4.

5.   *Treasure hunt*
Divide the children into teams of 4–5. Give each team a plastic bag and a list of objects to hunt for. Each team sets out in the school oval, or nearby park or beach, to collect the objects. Which team will finish the treasure hunt first with all the objects collected? Ensure the safety of the children.
VARIATIONS
Collect the objects in a given time. Which team can collect the most objects on the list?

5.

Combative fun activities

44

1.   *'Thread the needle'*
From stand tall position and fingers interlocked in front of you, lean over and try to put one leg through, then the other leg. Now reverse to your start position. Remember to keep your fingers interlocked throughout this activity!

1.

2. *Pull tug of war*
Partners stand face-to-face on one side of a line and grip right wrists. Partners try to pull each other over the line. Repeat using left wrist grip.

3. *Push tug of war*
Partners stand face-to-face with palms of hands touching. Partners push against each other's hands.

4. *'Knee box'*
With a partner stand face-to-face about a giant step apart in a 'home' space. On signal 'Knee box!' try to touch partner's knee without partner touching yours. Remember to stay in your home space. When you hear 'Knee box!' again, find a new partner to challenge!
VARIATION
Try to grab each other's tag belts or flags.

5. *Chinese get-up*
Partners long sit, back-to-back hooking elbows. Partners then try to stand up without breaking elbow-hold or using hands in any way. The idea is to gently push against each other's back and use legs to get to standing position. Emphasise that partners are about the same size.

5.

6. *Churn the butter*
Partners stand facing each other about a giant step apart and holding hands. Together partners, keeping the handhold, turn away from each other, back-to-back, around and facing again. Continue 'churning the butter' 2 more times. Repeat turning away from each other in the opposite direction.

7. *Partner snake roll*
Partners get into front-lying position, head-to-head, hands joined. Together partners roll in one direction, roll in the other direction, without breaking handhold.

7.

8. *Knee wrestle*
Face each other in kneeling position. Interlock hands and try to make the other lose their balanced position.

9. *Hoppo bumpo*
Partners about the same size take up a position with the left hand holding the right foot behind, while the right hand is used to gently push the other partner off balance. On signal 'Hoppo bumpo!' challenge a new partner and reverse handhold. Continue in this way.

10. *Turn the turtle*
Have your child lie down on their front and pretend to be 'glued' to the floor. You try to turn the 'turtle' over onto back. Then exchange roles. Be gentle, but strong as you attempt to turn the 'turtle' over!

11. *Arm wrestle*
Partners, facing in front-lying position on a soft surface, put up right forearms, while resting on upper arms, and grip hands. Each partner tries to arm wrestle the other by bringing the forearm to the floor. Repeat with left arm wrestle. Challenge someone else!

12. *Leg wrestle*
Partners get into back-lying position, hip-to-hip, positioning in opposite directions and hooking inside arms. On 'Go!' signal partners raise inside legs to a count of 3. On '3', partners try to wrestle the other's leg bringing it over to that partner's side. Right leg wrestle; then left leg wrestle. Challenge a new partner who is about the same size.

Action songs and ideas

45

Children love to move to music! Following are many simple ideas that involve moving to music using simple dance steps and actions or using a variety of rhythm equipment. Select music that has a lively beat and that is popular with the children. Better still, let the children choose the music.

Observe them in action, and watch for those smiles. They are contagious!

1. *If you're happy*
   A simple action song about showing emotions.

   If you're happy and you know it, clap your hands.
   If you're happy and you know it, clap your hands.
   If you're happy and you know it, then you really ought to show it.
   If you're happy and you know it, clap your hands.

   If you're angry and you know it, stamp your feet.
   If you're angry and you know it, stamp your feet.
   If you're angry and you know it, then your face is going to show it.
   If you're angry and you know it, stamp your feet.

   If you're sad and you know it, slowly turn around.
   If you're sad and you know it, slowly turn around.
   If you're sad and you know it, then your face is going to show it.
   If you're sad and you know it, slowly turn around.

   If you're sleepy and you know it, rub your eyes.
   If you're sleepy and you know it, rub your eyes.
   If you're sleepy and you know it, then your face is going to show it.
   If you're sleepy and you know it, rub your eyes.

2. *Hokey pokey*
   A simple traditional folk dance which teaches right and left body part recognition.

   You put your right foot in; you put your right foot out.
   You put your right foot in and you shake it all about.
   You do the hokey pokey and you turn yourself around.
   That's what it's all about.
   (Repeat with left foot, right hand, left hand, head, bottom, and so on)

3. *The wheels on the bus*

   The wheels on the bus go round and round, round and round, round and round.
   The wheels on the bus go round and round, all the way to town-o.
   (Children do gentle slow arm circles.)

   The wipers on the bus go swish, swish, swish . . .
   (Children move arms from side to side in a sweeping action.)

   The horn on the bus goes honk, honk, honk . . .
   (Children open and close hands.)

   The brakes on the bus go screech, screech, screech . . .
   (Children stamp their feet.)

The windows on the bus go up and down . . .
(Children rise up on toes, then sink down low.)

The lights on the bus go blink, blink, blink . . .
(Children open and close their eyes or blink with one eye then the other.)

The headlights on the bus beam bright, bright, bright;
bright, bright, bright; bright, bright, bright.
The headlights on the bus beam dim, dim, dim
All the way to home-o.
(Children slowly sink to the floor and pretend to go to sleep.)

4. *Let's go to the beach*
   (Make up instructions for the children to follow.) Grab your hat, sunnies and towel. (Mime the actions for this.) Jog along to the beach. Who wants to go swimming? Let's do the front crawl; let's do the backstroke; now do the breaststroke. Show me how you can tread water. Time to go snorkelling. Put on your mask, fins and snorkel in your mouth. Walk backwards into the water. And now we are snorkelling alone. Look at all the interesting sea creatures!

Crab (mime a crab walk action)

Octopus—gliding along

Shark—darting here and there

Seahorse—bobbing up and down

Stingray—gently flapping its wings

Dance fitness

1. *The Birdy dance*

   This popular novelty dance involves the basic steps of skipping and elbow swinging and is danced throughout the world by young and old! Have dancers pair off and form groups of 4. Each group finds a free space. In each group, one pair of dancers faces the other pair, about 2 giant steps apart. Check for good spacing. Use the 'Birdy dance' song available from major sports catalogue companies.

   PART A

   Cheep-cheep, cheep-cheep
   Imitate a bird's beak opening and closing by opening and closing fingers and thumb (4 counts)

   Flap-flap, flap-flap
   Imitate a bird flapping its wings by hooking thumbs under armpits and moving elbows up and down (4 counts)

   Wiggle-wiggle, wiggle-wiggle
   Imitate a bird ruffling its feathers by swaying hips from side to side (4 counts)

   Clap-clap, clap-clap
   Clap hands together (4 counts)

   PART B

   Swing-2-3-4-5-6-7-8
   Hook right elbows with partner and skip CW in a circle (8 counts)

   Swing-2-3-4-5-6-7-8
   Hook left elbows with partner and skip CCW in a circle (8 counts)

   Repeat from the beginning.

   VARIATION:

   Repeat Part B but, on the last 4 counts of the left elbow swing, everyone quickly form new groups of 4, partner up, ready to begin the 'Birdy dance' again.

CHEEP - CHEEP!

FLAP- FLAP!

WIGGLE-WIGGLE

CLAP-CLAP!

SWING 2-3-4--8

2. *Let's do the twist!*
   This was a song made popular by Chubby Checker and is available from most music stores.

   The twisting action is similar to 'towelling your backside and rubbing your feet into the ground!' Find a free space, listen to the music and twist away!
   • Twist from a high level to a low level. How low can you go?
   • Twist from a low level to a high level.
   • Twist with your feet together then gradually twist them further and further apart; gradually twist feet together again.
   • Twist and move sideways; twist around in a circle.
   • Jump up in the air, land and keep twisting again.
   • Don't forget to smile! ☺
   • Twist with a partner. Copy each other's twisting actions.
   • Twist away from each other; towards each other.
   • One partner twists CW while the other partner twists CCW.
   • One partner twist high the other low; vice versa.
   • Invent another twisting action with your partner.

3. *Splash!*
   Choose popular music with a steady 4/4 beat.

FRONT CRAWL   BACK STROKE

   16 counts: 'scrambled eggs—jog' jog in general space, in and out of each other
   8 counts: 'front crawl' while jogging in place
   8 counts: 'backstroke' while jogging in place
   Pause break: Hands on hips, feet together, push seat out to one side for 2 counts; repeat to other side. Say 'Splash' (raise hands in air) for 2 counts and clap! (2 counts)

BREAST STROKE

   16 counts: jog to the music in 'scrambled eggs' pattern
   8 counts: 'breaststroke' while jogging in place
   8 counts: 'backstroke' while jogging in place
   Pause break . . .

   16 counts: jog to the music in 'scrambled eggs' pattern
   8 counts: 'sidestroke' while jogging in place
   8 counts: 'backstroke' while jogging in place
   Pause break . . .

SIDESTROKE   BUTTERFLY

   16 counts: jog to the music in 'scrambled eggs' pattern
   8 counts: 'butterfly' while lightly bouncing in place
   8 counts: 'backstroke' while jogging in place
   Pause break . . .

TREADING WATER

   16 counts: 'treading water' by swaying arms in air, swaying legs in place; breathing gently to catch your breath—slowing down . . .!

4. *Hand jiving*
   This is a lively and enjoyable 'icebreaker' clapping routine. Teach at a slow tempo first, then pick up the tempo. Use a wave formation or a semi-circle formation and music with a steady 4/4 beat.

   HAND ACTIONS
   Pat thighs twice; clap hands twice

   Cross right; cross left
   Palms down, cross right hand over left twice.
   Then cross left hand over right twice.

   Hit right fist on left; hit left fist on right
   Make 2 fists, hit right fist on top of left twice.
   Then hit left fist on top of right twice.

   Touch right elbow and shake right pointer
   Touch left elbow and shake left pointer

   Lasso-2-3-4; lasso-2-3-4
   Circle right arm over head (4 counts)
   Circle left arm overhead (4 counts)

   Hitchhike-3-4; Hitchhike-3-4
   Point right thumb over right shoulder (4 counts)
   Point left thumb over left shoulder (4 counts)

   Grab a fly, put it in your hand, squish it, flick it away and stamp on it.
   Reach up in the air and catch an imaginary bug.
   Put it in the palm of your hand, squish it, flick it away and stamp on it.

   Repeat from beginning.

Rhythm fitness ideas

1. *The marching band*
   Children explore and create rhythms and rhythm patterns in personal and general space, using a variety of rhythm instruments. Form 3 groups:

   shakers (tambourines, maracas)

   strikers (drums, rhythm sticks)

   ringers (cymbals, triangles, wrist bells)

Children march in general space keeping in time to the music with their instruments and feet! On the loud drum beat, children change direction. On the whistle, children march in place and trade their instrument with someone else.

2. *The orchestra*

   Each group, shakers, strikers and ringers, collects in a certain area and creates a rhythm pattern that the group will play. Teacher/leader/parent is the 'conductor' and uses a conductor's baton (rhythm stick) to point and signal each group to play their rhythm pattern with the rhythm instruments. On the 'Cut!' signal with the baton, that group immediately stops. Explore bringing in different combinations: Groups 1 and 2; Groups 1 and 3; Groups 2 and 3; all 3 together; one group at a time.

3. *The pow-wow*

   Use Native Indian drumming music or aboriginal music. Have children cross-leg sit in one large circle, with each child holding a pair of rhythm sticks. Establish a drumming sequence. Choose a 'chief' to lead the group.

   VARIATIONS

   Split drummers into 3–4 groups and select a chief for each group. Each group creates its own drumming patterns. Groups may decide to add 'dance footwork' to their drumming.

4. *Rhythm sticks*

   Make rhythm sticks from dowelling cut into lengths of 30 cm (12 in). Have sticks painted as an art project, 2 sticks per child. Use music with a strong 4/4 beat. Each child finds a free space, knee-sits and explores creating different tapping patterns:
   • Tap sticks in front on floor, 2 counts
   • Tap sticks in air, 2 counts
   • Tap sticks in front on floor, 2 counts
   • Tap sticks in air, 2 counts
   • Alternate tapping sticks to each side, 2 counts

• Alternate tapping sticks in front, 2 counts
• Flip one stick, catch; flip the other stick, catch (4 counts)
Repeat pattern.

Now have children pair up with partners facing each other in knee-sit position.

4.

Create a tapping routine with your partner, for example:
• Tap sticks in front on floor, 2 counts
• Tap partner's sticks, 2 counts
• Tap sticks in front on floor, 2 counts
• Tap partner's sticks, 2 counts

5. *Rhythmic ribbons*
   • Purchase a set of ribbons from a sports catalogue or make rhythmic ribbons by attaching a 4–5 metres/yards length of satin or synthetic ribbon to a 50 cm long dowelling rod. Use a fishing line swivel and trace, screw-eye and about 30 cm (12 in) of fishing line to connect the parts as shown.
   • Keep the rod in line with the arm and hold the end in the palm with the pointer finger extended.
   • Keep ribbon moving continuously to create good flow.
   • Use a wrist movement for most ribbon patterns using the shoulder as the axis.
   • Emphasise taking good care of the ribbon and demonstrate how to wrap the ribbon for storage.
   • Check for good spacing so that ribbons do not become entangled.
   • Have children use dominant hand at first; then try ribbon patterns holding the ribbon in the non-dominant hand.
   • Add footwork to complement ribbon movement.
   • At the end ask children to wrap ribbons gently around the stick and put in storage.

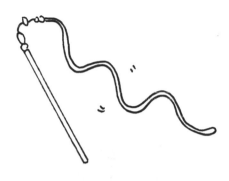

   SOME RIBBON ACTIONS
   • Windscreen wipers: swing ribbon from side to side
   • Traffic cops: swing ribbon back and forth
   • Helicopters: circle ribbon overhead
   • Propellers: circle ribbon in front
   • Wheels: circle ribbon at either side
   • Butterflies: swing in a figure-8 pattern in front
   • Bows: swing ribbon in figure-8 pattern at either side
   • Ribbons: swing ribbon in figure-8 pattern overhead
   • Coils: make bigger and bigger circles; then smaller and smaller circles
   • Zingers: make spirals from left to right; right to left
   • Air snakes: raise and lower arms to a wiggle pattern in the air
   • Floor snakes: lower arm and flick wrist to make ribbon wiggle along the floor
   • Create a ribbon action of your own!

WINDSHIELD WIPERS

TRAFFIC COPS

HELICOPTERS

BUTTERFLIES

Circuits

48

You can produce simple circuits in the home and together with children work through a number of activities. Music can be used to enhance the circuit activities and for timing.

The idea of a circuit is that children can either complete a certain number of attempts for each activity in a given target time or as fast as possible. Alternatively, the children can work for a set time and complete as many attempts as possible for each activity.

The target numbers should be obtained through initially observing how many trials can be completed in a set time, and then trying to better the score for that particular activity.

There are several other fitness activities in this book that can be incorporated into similar fitness circuits.

Following are 2 examples of a 5-station inside circuit. Not a lot of space is required for this circuit—in fact a normal room will provide ample space. Ensure the safety of the children at all times.

Inside circuit 1

1. *Rebound jogging*
   Jog lightly on rebounder or jump rope in place.

2. *Triangle run*
   Set up 3 markers or cones as shown and number them 1, 2 and 3. Runner starts at marker 1, runs around marker 2, back around 1, around marker 3 and back to touch marker 1. Record time.

3. *Balloon bat*
   Keep a balloon afloat by striking it gently with a small wooden bat.

4. *Wall sit*
   Lean your back against a wall while keeping your legs at right angles. Stay in this position.

5. *Box toss and run*
   Each player must toss a beanbag or ball into a large cardboard box (or plastic bucket or bin placed near a wall) then run to retrieve the beanbag and hand it to the next player who then tosses the beanbag and runs to fetch it. Gradually increase the distance as throwing skill improves.
   VARIATIONS
   • Hit ball off wall to rebound into cardboard box or bin.
   • Use underhand throw, then overhand throw.
   • Throw with best hand, then use other hand.

Inside circuit 2

1. *Locomotion rectangle*

   Mark out a rectangle 15 metres/yards by 10 metres/yards. Children move around the sides of the rectangle using different forms of locomotion. Set up a corner sign to indicate the type of movement to be used.

   For example: run forwards down side 1
   hop along the width (side 2)
   skip down side 3
   walk backwards along width (side 4)

2. *Ball swat*

   From a squatting position, child jumps up as high as possible to try to swat a ball in a hanging stocking. Earn a point each time you slap the ball. Remind child to bend knees on each landing!

3. *Long rope jumping*

   Children try to jump as many times as possible in the long rope.

4. *Beat the clock*

   Use pins or plastic jugs to mark out 4 clock positions: noon, 3, 6 and 9 o'clock. Mark the centre of the circle with an 'X' as shown. Each player, in turn, must run to knock over each clock pin position, returning to centre each time before knocking over the next clock pin. Players could record the time to complete the task for each other.

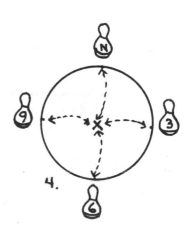

5. *Beam and crab walk*

   Children take turns sliding on their fronts from one end of the beam to the other, sliding off the end and crab walking back to the start of the beam.

   VARIATION

   Use a plank and have children 'walk' along it.

Outdoor fitness circuit

Below are suggestions for setting up an outdoor circuit using existing playground equipment.

Have child move against a set time or repeat activity a certain number of times.

When children are doing circuits do not expect them to improve every time. You should explain to children that sometimes they may not perform as well as the time before. This can be due to being tired or not feeling well on one day; or doing extra well on another day. Over time, improvement will occur.

Always try to ensure the safety of children. Teach them to be aware of moving safely and to respect the equipment they are using. Also spot or support them as necessary. Offer plenty of encouragement and praise for their efforts!

1. *Swing time*
   Take turns pushing each other on the swings or swing back and forth on a long fixed rope.

2. *Slide fun*
   Climb up the steps and slide down. Explore different ways of sliding down!

3. *Hand walk*
   Hand walk across the horizontal ladder.

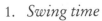

4. *Flying fox*
   Take turns hanging on and gliding across a flying fox frame.

5. *Hang tall*
   Hang with palms-down grip on a horizontal bar. With someone who can spot you properly, try to hang upside down.
   VARIATION
   Hang from rings.

6. *Monkey see, monkey do*
   Climb up, down, over and under, through the monkey bars or cargo net, then slide down the pole.

7. *Tunnel crawl*
   Crawl through the tunnel.

6.

7.

8. *Balance beam*
   Walk along the beam from one end to the other. Explore other ways of moving and balancing on the beam.

8.

Obstacle course

These are readily available in many parks and school grounds, but they can also be easily set up at home.

Here is an example of a home obstacle course.
- Climb a fence
- Run to the corner of the yard
- Walk across the bridge without falling in (1–2 m long × 5 cm wide length wooden beam)
- Hand-to-hand travel between or on the rungs of a ladder
- Hop between the markers
- Rope climb to a knot (rope suspended from a sturdy tree branch)
- Hang from a narrow beam

VARIATION
Together with children create another obstacle course that could be set up in a rumpus room in your house using chairs, tables, carpet squares, ropes, hoops, cushions, poles, music, and so on.

Marker obstacle course
Use hand prints, foot prints, directional arrows, squares, dome cones and sequencing spots to create a variety of obstacle courses. Let each group create its own course and have other groups go through it.

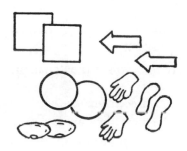

Concentration activities

1. *Pink panther*

   Use the theme music if possible. Select 2 children to be the 'pink panthers'. The rest are 'sleepers' who find a home space in the play area and get into back-lying position, with arms folded across chest and eyes closed. When the music starts, the pink panthers, keeping hands behind their backs, prowl around the area and bend down to talk to sleeping players. The pink panthers are encouraged to be clever and humorous as they try to get a sleeping player to wake up. If the sleeping player moves in any way, they are automatically awakened and become a pink panther helper trying to wake up other sleepers. The challenge is to see which sleeping player can last the length of the song and become the best concentrator(s) of the day!

2. *'Gotcha!'*

   Everyone sits in a large circle in cross-leg sit position quite near to the person on either side and with right thumb up and left hand flat and over the thumb of the person on your left (see illustration). Wait for my signal 'Gotcha!' It may be heard when you least expect it. Then on signal 'Gotcha!', try to grab the thumb of the person on your left while, at the same time, trying to pull your own thumb away from being caught.
   - Repeat with your eyes closed. Listen carefully for the signal.
   - Reverse so that left thumb is up; right hand is flat over the thumb of the person on your right.
   - Again repeat with eyes closed.

3. *Rock, paper, scissors*

   This is an ideal concentration activity to cool down the children after high energy output in performing more vigorous activities. Rules are simple: paper covers rock; rock crushes scissors; and scissors cut paper. Hand actions are simple, too:
   - 'Rock' is made by placing one fist on top of the other
   - 'Paper' by spreading one hand flat on top of bottom fist
   - 'Scissors' by spreading pointer and middle finger apart on top of bottom fist

   Children pair up and sit facing each other. On signal '1, 2, 3, show!' each child taps one fist on the other 3 times, then shows either 'rock', 'paper' or 'scissors' action. A win is decided, for example, if partner A shows 'paper' while partner B shows 'rock', then 'A' wins (since 'paper covers rock') and 'A' gets 1 point. Play to 5 points then challenge someone else.

4. *'Concentration, concentration'*

   This is an alertness, listening, concentration and cooperation activity. Children in groups of 8–10 sit cross-legged in a circle and number off 1, 2, 3 . . . 10. Number 1s are the leaders who start the activity. Children practise the slap–clap–snap rhythm first: slap knees twice, clap hands twice, then snap fingers. Keep rhythm steady and slow to moderate in tempo.

'SLAP – SLAP'
'CLAP – CLAP'
'1 – 2'

- Leader starts the rhythm: 'slap–slap; clap–clap; snap–snap.' Second time through on the 'snap–snap' leader calls out own number, then the number of another child in the group; for example 'slap–slap; clap–clap; '1 . . . 7'
- Now the child whose number has been called waits until the next 'snap–snap' and says their own number and the number of another child: '7 . . . 3' (you may call the number of the child who just called your number!)

VARIATION

Form groups of 6. Get 2 'lives' to stay in the game; then, if you say the wrong number sequence, you must sit out, but can still do the slap–clap–snap rhythm sequence. Now the challenge becomes for those players still in the game to remember the numbers left!

5. *The eye box*

On a large poster or flip chart draw a large rectangular box as shown. Tell the children that this is an 'eye box'. In the box using a different coloured marking pen indicate the following locations: top right, top middle, top left, bottom right, bottom middle, bottom left. Ask children to stand tall in a home space. Make sure that they can all see the eye box. Call out different locations and have each child move only their eyes to those places. Emphasise that they keep their heads still and move only their eyes. Observe their actions and comment.

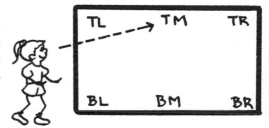

VARIATIONS

- For younger children use pictures of well-known animals.
- Use colours red, orange, yellow, green, blue and purple for the locations.
- Have each child draw their own eye box and then use it for letting their eyes move to the locations called.
- Now have them imagine an eye box in front of them. Call out different locations.

Juggling scarves play

A juggling scarf is made from a lightweight nylon material 45 cm × 60 cm (16 in × 24 in). These scarves will float in the air almost in slow motion, making it easy for the child to visually track. Also through juggling children can improve hand-eye coordination, manual dexterity, concentration, listening skills and peripheral vision.

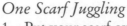

One Scarf Juggling

1. Put your scarf over a knee and grab it in the middle with the first three fingers of your favourite hand—'pincer grip'. Wave your scarf through the air as if it was a 'ghost'.

2. Toss your scarf upwards and let it settle down on a different body part each time. Toss with one hand; then toss with the other hand.

3. Using one hand toss your scarf upwards and wait as long as you can to grab it coming downwards before it touches the floor. Repeat using the other hand.

4. *Travelling scarves*
   • Swish your scarf through your legs in a figure-8
   • Sweep it like a windscreen wiper
   • Twirl it above your head like a helicopter blade
   • Circle it in front of you like a propeller
   • Swirl it in a large figure-8 in front of you
   • Create another way of making your scarf travel

WIPERS   HELICOPTERS   FIGURE-8s

4.

5. Toss your scarf across your body and let the other hand grab it with a downwards 'clawing' action.

Two scarves juggling

6. Start by holding 2 scarves in one hand, then toss one, toss the other, and keep this pattern going! Repeat with the other hand.

6.

7. Show me what other activities you can do with your scarf.

8. Toss both scarves in the air at the same time, then try to catch them.

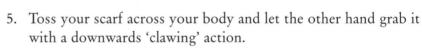

• Try to juggle with two scarves by tossing one across the body; then, at the peak of the first scarf, toss the second scarf. Grab downwards with the hand on that side. Cues: 'Toss–toss, grab–grab'.

8.

9. *Three scarves juggling*
    Hold the middle of first scarf in one hand using 'pincer grip'; hold the second scarf in the other hand using 'pincer grip'. Hold the third scarf with the fourth and fifth fingers of the favourite hand. This is the ready position. Now let's try juggling 3 scarves! Begin with the hand that holds 2 scarves.
    • Toss the first scarf across your body and above the opposite shoulder.
    • When this scarf gets to the top of the toss, send the second scarf above the opposite shoulder.
    • When the second scarf gets to the top of the toss, throw the third scarf across the body and above the opposite shoulder.
    • As a scarf falls downwards grab with the hand on that side and send it back across to the opposite side.
    • Continue this figure-8 pattern, alternating hands and using the cues: '1, 2, 3' or call out the colours of the scarves (pink, yellow, orange).
    • To learn the throwing order, toss the scarves and let them float to the floor, calling out the colours.

9.

VARIATIONS
• Windmill juggling.
• Toss the scarves as above, out with arm sweeping downwards and outwards, and then in towards the middle.